Designing Personalized Learning
FOR EVERY STUDENT

Dianne L. Ferguson
Ginevra Ralph
Gwen Meyer
Jackie Lester
Cleo Droege
Hafdís Guðjónsdóttir
Nadia Katul Sampson
Janet Williams

ASCD

Association for Supervision
and Curriculum Development

Alexandria, Virginia USA

Association for Supervision and Curriculum Development
1703 N. Beauregard St. • Alexandria, VA 22311-1714 USA
Telephone: 1-800-933-2723 or 703-578-9600 • Fax: 703-575-5400
Web site: http://www.ascd.org • E-mail: member@ascd.org

Printed in the United States of America.

ASCD Product No. 101007   s10/2001
ASCD member price: $18.95   nonmember price: $22.95

Library of Congress Cataloging-in-Publication Data

Designing personalized learning for every student / by Dianne L.
Ferguson ... [et al.].
        p. cm.
Includes bibliographical references and index.
    ISBN 0-87120-520-3 (pbk. : alk. paper)
    1. Individualized instruction. 2. Curriculum planning. 3.
Handicapped children—Education. I. Ferguson, Dianne L.
    LB1031 .D455 2001
    371.39'4—dc21
                                        2001005809

06 05 04 03 02 01   10 9 8 7 6 5 4 3 2 1

Designing Personalized Learning for Every Student

List of Figures

Preface

This book reflects a decade and a half of collaboration and learning among groups of educators trying to improve their teaching practices in the face of dizzying changes. The book began in 1986, when a university professor (Ferguson) first invited a group of teachers to talk about their work, the challenges they faced, and the changes they might wish to pursue. This teacher work group included two of the authors (Meyer and Ralph), who have been part of the development, implementation, and evaluation of these ideas since that first meeting. This first work group and subsequent ones wrote the ideas in this book as modules and revised them as the teachers involved changed, learned, and developed—adding new ideas, new voices, and new results from teachers in Oregon (Droege, Lester, and Williams), other states, and even other countries (Guðjónsdóttir).

Each revised set of ideas was used and evaluated not only by the teachers involved in the work groups, but also by those in teacher education programs at the University of Oregon (Sampson) and by hundreds of others who participated in a series of federally funded professional development, research, and outreach projects. Teachers in all levels and sizes of schools in all kinds of settings took the ideas, tried them out, and provided reactions, results, and revisions. Teachers still report how they use, adopt, and adapt the book's central ideas:

- All children and youth are learners.
- Learning must help children and youth become more competent and contributing members of their current and future communities.

• All students learn differently and bring a variety of differences to the learning enterprise—from differences in ability, language, and culture to differences in family situations, ways of learning, personal and financial resources, and interests and passions.

• Teachers must creatively and continually tailor learning and outcomes to each student, while directing all students toward important community learning goals and standards.

• All students, regardless of the unique signatures they bring to learning, can achieve these goals and standards in their own way and contribute to their community.

This book presents what these groups of teachers have learned about how to make these ideas work in classrooms. Some of the teachers began as special educators, hoping to achieve better participation and learning outcomes for students whom the school system had designated as needing special education. Students ranged from those who needed a little extra time or attention to those with significant and multiple disabilities. In working with one another, these special educators became a new breed of educator, able to negotiate the language and practices of general education while ensuring achievement for students with disabilities and other differences that might present barriers to learning. Other teachers started out as general educators and acquired new capacities to accommodate a wider diversity of students in ways that resulted in high levels of achievement.

The "cross-pollination" of the general and special educators create in this book a synthesis

of learning and professional development. We think this synthesis finally undoes the results of the separation of general and special education. These teachers and these ideas combat what Seymour Sarason (1990) has described as the all-too-common consequence of traditional teacher education:

> School personnel are graduates of our colleges and universities. It is there that they learn there are at least two types of human beings, and if you choose to work with one of them you render yourself legally and conceptually incompetent to work with others. (p. 258)[1]

We would like to acknowledge our university colleagues, our critics, and all the general and special educators who have contributed in large and small ways to the ideas and tools in this book. These contributors are now the new hybrid educators who are engaged in reinventing schools into unified systems, where all teachers and every student contribute to the learning and growth of the community of schooling.

Special thanks go to Audrey Desjarlais for coordinating meetings and communications among the authors, providing technical support, and preparing book chapters for editing.

---

[1]Sarason, S. (1990). *The Predictable Failure of Educational Reform.* San Francisco: Jossey-Bass.

Introduction

Changes are everywhere in today's schools. Teachers are reexamining how and what they teach. Administrators and school boards are experimenting with innovative management strategies. University educators are refocusing their research and theories to better describe effective teaching and learning as students and teachers experience it. Daily reports in the media urge changes in all aspects of schooling for all types of students and teachers.

At the same time, students are more diverse—in cultural backgrounds, learning styles and interests, social and economic classes, and abilities and disabilities. Successfully including students with so many differences and different ways of learning challenges schools to reinvent themselves as more flexible, creative learning communities that include and are responsive to a full range of human diversity. This newly defined diverse norm replaces the old statistically derived, bell-shaped-curve norm that uncompromisingly identifies some students as "inside" and others as "outside."

With this shift in norm definition, a parallel shift in teacher work becomes possible. Until recently, the mission of special education has been to find and try to repair those aspects of students' learning that cause students to fall outside the norm, so that they might once again become part of the "in-group." A task for general educators has been to assist this agenda by identifying those students who do not seem to fit into that group, so that special educators can determine why and try to change the special education designation for those students.

The logic of diversity and inclusiveness frees both groups of teachers from the task of seeking out and naming student learning differences and deficits. Instead, teachers can focus on creating and tailoring curriculum and teaching so that schooling works for every student.

What Is the Purpose of Schooling?

It is easy to get confused about what schooling is supposed to accomplish for students, especially in these fast-changing times. Too much of what educators do every day can easily become caught up in rules, tests, regulations, scores, and grades. Although these concerns have their importance and roles, they often serve to obstruct education's mission. Whatever details teachers must address, the real purpose of schooling for any student, no matter how able or disabled, is simple: to enable all students to actively participate in their communities so that others care enough about what happens to them to look for ways to incorporate them as members of that community.

Of course, each student will learn different knowledge to accomplish this outcome. But the point of school is not so much what students learn as what that learning allows them to accomplish as members of the community in which they live.

Are Any Schools Accomplishing This Purpose?

Many schools are accomplishing this purpose for many different kinds of students. Nevertheless, educators do not yet know much about how to attain it for *every* student. Throughout the United States and other countries, schools are just now starting the process of reinventing themselves to accomplish this more student-oriented agenda. Such work requires that our schools bring together the talents and practices of previously separate educational programs to form a unified system that can flexibly respond to these new demands.

A unified educational system is based on the principle that each student represents a unique combination of abilities and educational needs and deserves individual help at various times throughout schooling to achieve important outcomes. Key to this belief is the idea that schools are organized around learning supports, not programs and services. In a unified educational system, all types of resources provide learning supports in a range of settings to students with unequal educational needs. Teachers share accountability for all students—those from low-income homes, with disabilities, with limited English proficiency, and from different racial and cultural backgrounds—and ensure that all students are effectively educated.

In a successful unified system, educators believe not only that all students can learn, but also that, collectively, educators are capable of teaching all students. As a result, the lines between general education, special education, Title I, bilingual education, migrant education, vocational education, and other categorical programs become blurred and eventually disappear. Previously separate programs for specific groups of students come together to form a new educational system. Such a system anchors its work in standards of student-learning content, performance, and skills that are valued by local communities and families and informed by national and state standards, curriculum frameworks, and assessment strategies.

Reinventing and Unifying School Systems

The task of reinventing and unifying educational systems is complex, but it is often made more so by the sheer number of demands for change that schools and teachers must field. Change tasks are also often different sizes. Some can be understood and mastered in a relatively short time. Others require a lengthy effort, in part because they seek to change more fundamental ways of thinking and working in schools. Too often, the task overload many educators experience can turn important and fundamental changes into small, quick fixes that change little. Some change demands seem contradicted by other change demands, at least on the surface. Of course, some changes really are in conflict, but others are not

when they are better understood.

One way to handle the number and variety of changes required to become a school for the future is to organize efforts meaningfully. The systemic change framework (see Figure I.1) helps to structure and network change efforts at district, school, and classroom levels. Schools are learning that when they are organized around the capacity to change, their systems look different from the traditional district and school bureaucracies that have been organized for efficiency and stability.

The systemic change framework shows the levels of effort that combine to affect student achievement and learning: district, school, professional, and student. These levels of effort are interconnected; what occurs at the district level affects the school level, which ultimately affects student learning. All of this work occurs within the context of family and community. The lines separating the levels and the components within each level are linked by this context. When efforts at the three outer levels are maximized—that is, they are in sync with one another—the result is a healthy system that can better support student learning.

The framework begins with student learning as the core of all school effort. We believe that student learning needs to be defined in a broad context that includes self, social, career, and academic knowledge and competence. For learning to occur, students must act or expend effort; therefore, the inner circle of the framework represents student effort.

Although student learning is a school's most important outcome, such learning comes from

I.1 The Systemic Change Framework

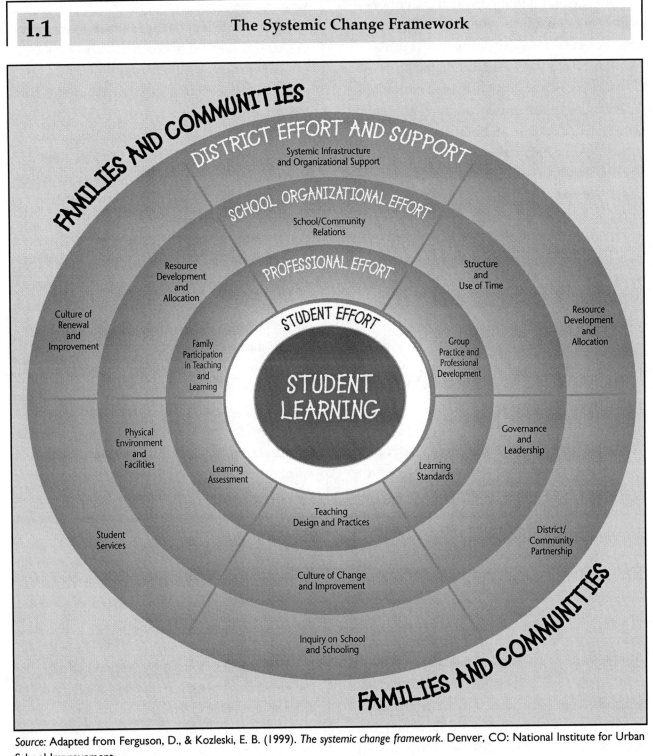

Source: Adapted from Ferguson, D., & Kozleski, E. B. (1999). *The systemic change framework.* Denver, CO: National Institute for Urban School Improvement.

individual and group efforts that are only partially accounted for by school-controlled factors. As a result, schools must focus their attention on providing the conditions, opportunities, tasks, role models, relationships, and information that support and nurture student learning. This focus requires thoughtful, caring, and reflective practice in classrooms that are supported by buildingwide systems for professional development and resource stewardship. The restructuring and renewal work in which schools must engage then becomes more manageable by grouping elements of that work into clusters. The framework provides a common language for school professionals, whose specializations often create barriers to common interests. Because these elements describe the work of teaching students with and without disabilities or other differences, schools can integrate inclusive practices with other reform goals to form a coherent approach to change and renewal of educational processes.

The Changing Face of Schools

We offer this framework as a beginning for this book because it helps to organize the different demands for change that schools face. The focus of the book, however, is to offer ideas and strategies at the level of professional effort. We have written this book for teachers, who may be the most important architects of reinvented unified schools. Our intent is to help teachers create curriculum and teaching that will accommodate the widest possible student diversity, including students who are officially designated as disabled. The ideas in this book apply to any student.

We use a fictitious teacher, Ms. Clark, her 6th grade language arts block class, her thinking about her class, and her work with other teachers as the source for the stories and examples we weave throughout the book. These stories do not come from just one class, of course, but have been collected from the many teachers and students that have been part of the book's development. We have created Ms. Clark's class as a way of making all these experiences come together into a situation that we hope will look familiar to readers. Ms. Clark, her school and school district, her students, and her professional associates are fictitious, but they represent realistic people in realistic situations.

This book is best used in combination with other curriculum and teaching materials that emphasize preferred practices for whatever kinds of students teachers must teach. We recommend applying the ideas to students that teachers may think do not fit into the typical classroom, such as students with disabilities, challenging behavior, or difficult family and emotional needs. These are the types of students who prompt teachers to think that whatever the current change agenda, it surely does not apply to them. We also suggest additional resources in each chapter that you can pursue to learn more about the main ideas and ways to apply these ideas to students with other kinds of differences.

Three Big Ideas

In trying to blend the innovations already occurring within both general and special education, we have designed an approach to student assessment, curriculum design, and planning of teaching that responds to a variety of dilemmas teachers face. This approach rests on thinking differently about how teachers work together, the roles of general and special educators, and the purpose and use of individualized education plans.

Locate Decisions with Groups of Teachers

No single teacher, no matter how experienced or gifted, is likely to possess all the knowledge, skills, and judgments required to effectively design curriculum and teaching experiences for the full range of student diversity. Some students with disabilities, for example, might require specialized supports in all areas of learning; others might require innovative and creative consideration in only a few specific areas.

We think that groups of teachers with *different* abilities and skills can together design effective and individually tailored learning experiences for all children. Some teachers need to be skillful at teaching traditional academic content. Others need to create learning activities that offer a wide range of learning opportunities across learning content areas. Still others need to effectively adapt and expand learning experiences for those students who learn differently or who have unique preferences about their learning—for example, they're only interested in learning about bugs, or in playing on the basketball team. Some students who have disabilities may require some kinds of learning over others. For example, learning how to use limited communication skills may take priority for awhile over science and math. Each teacher group will also sometimes need the even more specialized knowledge of other educational personnel who can help them design and deliver communication, behavioral, physical, and medical supports for students.

Create New Roles for Teachers

Throughout the history of special education, educators have developed a way of working in schools that places boundaries around what a teacher, or any other adult working in schools, can do. "General education" teachers teach "general" students—those in the middle of the bell-shaped-curve norm—because that is whom they were trained to teach. "Special education" teachers work with "special" students who have special learning needs, usually because they have some identified disability or fall outside the middle of the bell-shaped norm. This matching of teacher work to student characteristics is most elaborate for educational specialists. Physical therapists work with legs and whole bodies; occupational therapists, with hands and sometimes mouths; and speech therapists, with mouths, sounds, speech, and language. In every case, teachers are constrained by their training to do only certain things with those students who fit the training.

In reinvented schools, teachers may still have unique knowledge and skills about content areas, teaching strategies, or student supports. But all teachers indeed all adults in the school can teach diverse groups of students. Although a particular teacher might have been trained originally to provide communication supports, the other teachers on her team can support her in teaching literacy, or perhaps numeracy as well. The new role for *all* adults in schools is *teacher*.

Redesign the Individualized Education Plan (IEP)

The individualized education plan (IEP), as defined by educators, made sense when the approach to schooling for students who didn't fit the old bell-shaped-curve norm was to design a plan just for them. The logic of labeling or naming what is wrong to provide help (i.e., the evaluation and classification system in special education) also requires that we design a specific plan that tries to fix what is wrong. To do less would mean that we single out some children as "not okay" and leave them with the dishonor and stigma of being found lacking. A newly conceived norm that includes all students means that this reason for a specific plan (the IEP) doesn't exist anymore. If we do not identify some children as lacking, there is less of a moral and legal requirement to do something to justify affixing that label.

On the other hand, for all students to achieve the schooling outcome of active, meaningful participation in their community, they must each receive an education that has been uniquely tailored or *personalized* to their abilities, interests, and communities. This kind of personalized

learning is another way to understand the requirements of individualized education plans, but how such plans function in schools is less clear.

Personalized learning isn't as challenging as it might sound. Teachers in general education are always tinkering with their lesson activities and assignments to tailor them to different students. This book describes a process for individually tailoring curriculum and learning so that *every* student has a unique learning experience that serves the student's growth, competence, and community participation.

Organization of This Book

Chapter 1 presents an overall framework for thinking about curriculum design that applies to any student. We emphasize the dynamic decision-based nature of curriculum and challenge teachers to embrace this decision-making responsibility as a critically important part of their work.

Chapter 2 focuses on a series of steps to gather information about students and to design and plan instructional activities that will create individually tailored learning experiences. If teachers must decide for every student how personalized learning should be organized and constructed, they need to know their students well. Our assessment approach complements more familiar assessments about what students know and can do by helping teachers learn who their students are.

Chapter 3 is an extended example of how one teacher, Ms. Clark, uses the assessment strategies described in Chapter 2 not only to get to know her students, but also to engage their families in the teaching and learning enterprise. She enlists family members to help design curriculum and teaching and achieves a better link between school learning and her students' lives outside school.

Chapter 4 offers ideas and tools teachers can use to plan units and lessons that will both help each student learn what needs to be learned and systematically factor in the kinds of support, assistance, and opportunity each will need to succeed. We illustrate these ideas and tools with an example of a teaching unit that Ms. Clark and her colleagues created.

Chapter 5 expands on the planning ideas presented in Chapter 4 by discussing ways to creatively and effectively group diverse students so that their different learning abilities, goals, and needs for support are addressed without creating logistical and management nightmares for teachers.

Finally, Chapter 6 presents ongoing recording and reporting formats teachers can use to share their decisions and student achievement with all those who might need or want to know about them. We also provide a framework for thinking about and organizing all the new demands and approaches to accountability and assessment that face today's teachers.

Each chapter includes examples of tools that teachers have developed and used to apply the ideas in this book daily in classrooms. Most of these tools are designed to be heuristic; that is, we designed them to help teachers *think* about their curriculum and teaching decisions. Many

teachers may only need to see the format to change their thinking-through practices. Others may need to fill out forms they've designed from our examples to practice the ideas and then use them for notes. Some forms and formats become a key part of some teachers' daily practice. Teachers may not need to actually write anything, but just keep the documents handy to look at when planning and thinking so they do not forget to consider all the relevant dimensions and can thus make better decisions.

For each broad procedural component (gathering information, planning, designing, and reporting), we provide ways to think through decisions and to evaluate whether or not the use of these ideas captures their fundamental logic. We also describe how each procedural component would function if a school is not yet completely "reinvented." We think that teachers, using some of these ideas, will affect how quickly schools become effective learning environments for *all* children and youth.

Meet Ms. Clark's 6th Grade Class

On any given day, as you approach Room 6, you might encounter a student or a small group in the hallway reading aloud or having a lively discussion about which book they should choose for an upcoming project. As you enter, you hear the controlled noise of student conversation coming from several groups scattered around the room. One group lounges comfortably on two old couches, listening to a book on tape and following along in their books. Another group sits on the floor talking. Another is crowded around a desk close to the three computers in the room. Near the front of the room, Ms. Clark sits with four students discussing another book. She briefly looks up when Ms. Jackson, the speech-language specialist, leads another group of five students out of the room to take advantage of an empty (and quiet) space next door, where the teacher is out of the room during her prep period.

The class is part of Grandview Middle School in the Willamette School District. Although fictitious, this school and district reflect the realities of many schools and districts throughout the United States. Grandview uses block classes of three periods (a total of 2 hours) for each grade level, supporting their middle school philosophy of integrating reading, social studies, and language arts. During the first 45 minutes of the 2-hour reading/language arts/social studies block class, Ms. Clark organizes the class's work into literature circles. The book the members have chosen to read organizes and focuses each literature circle.

While you wait to catch a few minutes with Ms. Clark, you wander around the room. You walk over to the students near the computers and listen to their discussion. You are surprised to hear them talking about the death of their pets, but more struck by how they are anxiously waiting to tell their story. "Is this on-task behavior?" you wonder. You glance at the cover of their book, hoping to gain a clue about how this topic of conversation related to their reading. You remain mystified until one student relates

the death of his pet to the death of an animal in the story. Another group is discussing each member's final projects. Evidence of other projects— posters, dioramas, mobiles, bulletin boards with student work, and computer-generated story webs with text and graphs—is scattered around the room.

A Bit of Context

About 10 years ago, the Willamette School District made a decision to bring back all special education students they had been placing in self-contained classrooms in a nearby district. At that time, the budget and overall student enrollment in this community meant that class sizes were small, about 18–20 students in most classrooms, each with various people and material resources available. Over the ensuing 10 years, finances diminished, student enrollments increased, and new students brought many more differences and needs. More Hispanic and Asian students began moving into the community. Changes in the local economy and an increasing unemployment rate created new challenges for families.

Today, teachers face larger classes, and it seems that none of the students are part of the typical middle group the teachers had long relied upon. Instead, each student brings significant learning differences and needs that challenge teacher creativity and capacity.

Toward the end of each year, teachers of all transitioning 5th grade students in the district prepare information to pass along to teachers at the middle school. At the middle school, Ms. Jackson (the speech-language specialist),

Ms. Simpson (the reading specialist), Ms. Clark, and Ms. Hendricks (a special education teacher) meet to discuss and plan ways to support the learning needs of the incoming group of 6th grade students. Ms. Jackson has previously worked with many of Ms. Clark's new students because she teaches at various elementary schools. She brings much useful information to the group. As they review the transition information prepared by the 5th grade teachers, ideas begin to fly about groupings they can try, reading support strategies, lesson accommodations, and more.

Meet Ms. Clark's Students

Mary, Bill, Sondra, and Audrey are considered typical students. Each excels in different ways. Mary and Sondra love to read and often exchange books. They frequently ask for extra credit assignments, and Ms. Clark usually offers them several options. Occasionally they perform short skits based on a particular scene or chapter in a book they have both read.

Bill and Audrey are both athletic and participate in many extracurricular activities. They spend their lunch breaks playing basketball or soccer with another group of Ms. Clark's students, Jamal, Val, Rhonda, Lydia, Darren, and Willis.

All these students typically turn in their homework, though they sometimes need prodding. They generally attend regularly and, for the most part, are able to complete their assignments on time with a little help from Ms. Clark or other adults working in the room. Ms. Clark tries to make sure she encourages each of them to take on extra assignments or work with other students who may need assistance. She doesn't want to overlook them because they don't demand a lot of specialized attention.

Ms. Clark uses a coffee can and Popsicle sticks labeled with students' names, and every day she pulls different names out of the can to call on students for answers to her questions. This way she is sure that all her students are given an opportunity to participate, and she is able to check for their understanding of the presented material. The students like the randomness and think it's fair.

Maria arrived from Mexico, speaking no English, to enter 3rd grade. No one speaks English at her home even three years later, but Maria has acquired a beginning English vocabulary. She is quiet, even a bit withdrawn at times, but caring toward other students. She has been identified as having a language disability, and she receives additional learning support from a special educator for oral and written language tasks, along with services for English as a Second Language (ESL) learners.

Miguel's English skills have been progressing well, with good support offered at home, partly because his parents joined a district parent support program targeting at-risk families. He is athletic and involved in soccer. He still receives ESL support, but may not need it much longer.

Jamie is also Hispanic, but he struggles to read, and most kids in the class read better than he does. Jamie was homeless for three years, living on the streets in a large city in the Northwest. He just reentered the school system and is currently living with his aunt. Jamie has not yet learned to decode or encode, which makes reading especially hard, but he possesses practical survival knowledge. He receives support from a special educator in all areas, even though he is not officially labeled. During his homeless years, Jamie did not attend school, a deprivation that has dramatically affected his academic progress. He is also finding it tough to fit into the social scene.

Jill is a quiet student from a single-parent home. Her achievements are modest, almost low average. Daily classwork is a struggle. She is inconsistent about doing homework and often arrives at school early hoping to find Ms. Clark available to help. Jill's mother works nights for the local Wal-Mart, and Jill must take care of several younger siblings while her mom works. These demands are probably why Jill has trouble doing homework at home and also why she appears tired most days. Although Jill is not interested in extracurricular activities or sports, she is fascinated by fashion, admiring the latest fashions and artificial nails.

Brandon's supportive family is a big help to him despite his struggles to learn. His reading is not fluent and reflects achievements more like many 2nd grade students. He has been identified with a learning disability since 1st grade. Although reading is hard for him, he comprehends well and can demonstrate his comprehension with wonderful artistic renderings and graphic mind maps. He is fascinated with insects, always choosing books focusing on this passion. Brandon is popular with his peers and is involved with sports and social activities.

Nadine is also well liked by her peers, always offering to lend a helping hand. Her reading fluency is poor, but she can comprehend what she has read or listened to. Her written language is improving slowly, perhaps in part because her expressive language skills are also weak. She qualifies for special education services in oral and written language.

Eli, Mark, Amanda, and Anna previously received Title I support and still benefit from extra support and exposure to language-rich experiences. Their reading levels are slightly behind their peers. They rarely complete written products and homework, which seem to be too hard for them to think about with much optimism.

Katie, Josiah, and Josh all have learning difficulties that require medication. Katie has been diagnosed with attention deficit disorder (ADD) and a language disorder. She reads fluently but has trouble comprehending what she reads, probably because of her difficulty in focusing on what she is reading. Her medication helps, but she frequently refuses to take it. Her supportive parents are eager to help. As professionals, they create a language-rich home environment.

Josiah and Josh can be quite challenging for their teacher and peers because of their behaviors, which are typical for students with attention deficit hyperactivity disorder (ADHD). Josiah wants to please. He comes to class chanting his mantra, "I'm going to be good, I'm going to be good," but is never quite able to pull it off. His parents struggle to manage his medication and health routines, and his home life seems more chaotic than supportive. Other students tend to avoid him because his clothes are unkempt, his hygiene is poor, and his social communications are often inappropriate and confusing to others.

Josh is a musician, constantly drumming rhythms, usually during inappropriate times. He is a fluent reader with great comprehension, but he is so disorganized with his belongings and thoughts that it's difficult to tell what's going on with him and what he knows or is learning. Josh has a large family and his mom is pulled in many directions, often seeming as disorganized as her son.

Ben is a serious student, intent on always doing his best. His attendance is perfect, and his classroom work and homework are always neatly done and turned in on time. He does excellent work, often the best in the class. His parents own a local Asian restaurant. Ben doesn't participate in after-school activities because everyone helps at the restaurant; Ben helps most afternoons and evenings. It is difficult for Ben's parents to come to school conferences or activities because of their busy work schedule. Ms. Clark also thinks they may be self-conscious about their limited English-speaking skills.

Susannah has Down syndrome. She has been assigned to a general education classroom since she entered the school system. Always social and even popular, Susannah is finding it harder to be socially involved in a middle school. She participates in choir and step aerobics and would like to do more sports if she had the time. She is a fluent reader but has poor comprehension of what she reads. Her single-parent mother is supportive of her social and academic life. But Susannah's mom is concerned about how well

Susannah will fit in socially as she progresses through the secondary grades.

Tasha is African American and has significant mobility disabilities because of cerebral palsy. She receives speech-language services for stuttering and occupational therapy for mobility support. Tasha has many interesting skills that contribute to the overall capacity of the class. She loves poetry and has a beautiful singing voice. She is outspoken and demonstrates strong leadership skills. Tasha's single-parent mom is supportive and tries to be involved in planning for Tasha's education. Currently, she is concerned about Tasha fitting into the middle school's social structure.

Becky is academically gifted but has problems with social relationships. She has a hard time sharing ideas and opinions when she is working in groups, though she usually has much to offer the group and tries to be generally helpful to other students. Students like her and appreciate her skills and knowledge, but they find her bossy and not able to share. Some students don't like to be in a group with Becky.

Samuel is also academically gifted, though he is somewhat shy. Students realize that he knows things, but don't really know how to help him express himself, especially in group activities. Samuel's parents would like to see him involved in more social and recreational activities, but he hangs back. His special passions are geography and history.

Tara is a vivacious student who loves the social life of middle school. Her mother is an elementary teacher, and her father is a coach in the Willamette School District. Tara is usually engaged in classroom activities, but she sometimes needs clear reminders and deadlines for class work and homework because her constant socializing with peers seems to distract her. She participates in many social activities and plays several sports. Tara's parents support the teacher's insistence that Tara take increased responsibility for her schoolwork, and they try to set similar limits and conditions at home.

Ms. Clark's Professional Friends

Ms. Clark is not alone in trying to meet the diverse needs of her students. She and her students benefit from support given by Ms. Jackson (the speech-language specialist), Ms. Simpson (the reading specialist), Ms. Muir (an ESL specialist), Ms. Hendricks (a special education teacher), Mr. Patterson (an occupational therapist), Mr. West (the librarian/media specialist), Ms. Dean (an educational assistant), parent and community volunteers, and occasional practicum students from a local university. Of course, all these adults are not always in Ms. Clark's classroom. They apportion their time across many classrooms, but always according to what is being taught and what learning needs students have. The scheduling can be incredibly complex, but everyone at Grandview tries to stay flexible.

These support educators take on many roles in Ms. Clark's classroom, from team-teaching the whole group to working with individual students. The students think of all these adults as *teachers*, no matter what their official title might be. Some students spend more time with some teachers than with others, depending upon their learning needs and the individual teacher's skills, but there are no rules about which teachers may (or may not) work with individual students. In fact, the groupings of teachers and students change, sometimes from day to day. The teachers who make up the team blend their knowledge and skills to benefit the entire class and contribute to each student's learning. Because the teachers have worked together to design the curriculum for the class, they feel connected to this learning community, and each has a strong commitment to maximizing the outcomes of their joint efforts. Ms. Clark, her students, and her colleagues illustrate the ideas in this book throughout the remaining chapters. We hope their experiences are familiar and helpful.

For Further Reading

Here are some helpful background readings you might want to pursue. The monograph by Dewey (1938) reflects on changes in the 1930s, but has messages that are salient today. The works by Ferguson (1995) and by Fullan and Steigelbauer (1991) offer different syntheses of school change that educators are now encountering. The stories by Kozol (1991) help place the overall task of school change in dramatic perspective by taking a close look at some of our poorest and most challenged schools. Goodlad has been a leader in school change and renewal. His three publications (1998, 1999a, 1999b) are a good introduction to his ideas.

The two brief publications by Ferguson (1999a, 1999b) discuss teacher preparation and ongoing professional development, both of which, we think, are essential to good inclusive schooling. They can be downloaded at the National Institute for Urban School Improvement's Web site at http://www.edc.org/urban.

The three publications by Elmore (1995, 1996a, 1996b) discuss the complexities of educational reform and how to make reform reach as many students and educators as possible. The two articles by Sizer (1984, 1997) discuss reform, the risks of maintaining the status quo, and the work of challenging our old ways. High school teachers will find them particularly interesting.

The publication by Irvine (1997) discusses how to build schools and educate youth in ways that honor, build on, and involve all students as citizens. It also includes information about the importance of preparing teachers with multicultural and democratic competence. These ideas may be particularly valuable for teachers in urban or other settings where student populations are diverse.

The book by Delpit (1995) and the April 1999 issue of *Educational Leadership* focusing on race, class, and culture, offer examples that educators may find helpful when they are figuring out ways to accommodate students with different cultural norms.

Delpit, L. (1995). *Other people's children: Cultural conflict in the classroom.* New York: W. W. Norton.

Dewey, J. (1938). *Experience and education.* New York: Macmillan.

Elmore, R. (1995). Structural reform and educational practice. *Educational Researcher, 24*(9), 23–26.

Elmore, R. (1996a). Getting to scale with good educational practice. *Harvard Educational Review, 6*(1), 1–26.

Elmore, R. (1996b). *Restructuring in the classroom: Teaching, learning, and school organization.* San Francisco: Jossey-Bass.

Ferguson, D. L. (1995). The real challenge of inclusion: Confessions of a "rabid inclusionist." *Phi Delta Kappan, 77*(4), 281–287.

Ferguson, D. L. (1999a). *On teacher preparation and support in inclusive schools.* Denver, CO: National Institute for Urban School Improvement.

Ferguson, D. L. (1999b). *On reinvented inclusive schools: A framework to guide fundamental change.* Denver, CO: National Institute for Urban School Improvement.

Fullan, M., & Steigelbauer, S. (1991). *The new meaning of educational change.* (2nd ed.). New York: Teachers College Press.

Goodlad, J. I. (1998). Schools for all seasons. *Phi Delta Kappan, 79*(9), 670–671.

Goodlad, J. I. (1999a). Flow, eros, and ethos in educational renewal. *Phi Delta Kappan, 80*(8), 571–578.

Goodlad, J. I. (1999b). Teachers as moral stewards of our schools. *Journal for a Just and Caring Education, 5*(3), 237–241.

Irvine, J. J. (1997). *Critical knowledge for diverse teachers and learners.* Washington, DC: American Association of Colleges for Teacher Education.

Kozol, J. (1991). *Savage inequalities: Children in America's schools.* New York: Crown Publishing.

Scherer, M. (Ed.). (1999). Understanding race, class, and culture. *Educational Leadership, 56*(7).

Sizer, T. (1984). *Horace's compromise: The dilemma of the American high school.* Boston: Houghton Mifflin.

Sizer, T. (1997). Horace's frustration, Horace's hope. *English Journal, 86*(5), 20–24.

Recommended Web Sites

http://www.essentialschools.org   The Coalition of Essential Schools is a growing national network of more than 1,000 schools and 24 regional support centers. The organization works to increase student achievement by supporting the rethinking of priorities and the redesign of curriculum, instruction, and assessment.

http://www.edc.org/FSC/ATLAS ATLAS Communities is a break-the-mold design linking elementary, middle, and high school pathways as partners in creating a consistent, personalized education in which all children achieve.

http://www.edc.org/urban The National Institute for Urban School Improvement's mission is to support inclusive urban communities, schools, and families to build their capacity for sustainable, successful urban education. The institute will accomplish this mission through dialogue, networking, technology, action research, information systems, alliance, and consensus building.

The network of 10 regional educational laboratories, serving geographic regions that span the United States, works to ensure that those involved in educational improvement at the local, state, and regional levels have access to the best available information from research and practice. Each laboratory has a Web site:

- http://www.lab.brown.edu/
  Northeast and Islands Regional Educational Laboratory at Brown University (The LAB at Brown University)

- http://www.temple.edu/lss/
  Laboratory for Student Success (LSS)

- http://www.ael.org/
  Appalachia Educational Laboratory (AEL)

- http://www.serve.org/
  The Regional Educational Laboratory at Serve

- http://www.ncrel.org/
  North Central Regional Educational Laboratory (NCREL)

- http://www.sedl.org/
  Southwest Educational Development Laboratory (SEDL)

- http://www.mcrel.org/
  Mid-continent Research for Education and Learning (McREL)

- http://www.wested.org/
  West Ed

- http://www.nwrel.org/
  Northwest Regional Educational Laboratory (NWREL)

- http://www.prel.org/
  Pacific Resources for Education and Learning (PREL)

A Framework for Curricular Design

What do teachers think of when they hear the word curriculum? A book for students? A workbook? A teacher's manual? A list of subjects they have to teach? Many teachers think of curriculum in one of these ways. To them, curriculum refers to what educators teach, and that information is determined by someone else (or some group) and given to them in the form of books, texts, and lists.

The Role of the "Official" Curriculum

Many countries, states, and districts have identified what might be called an "official" or "standard" *curriculum*. Externally imposed standards of achievement or student outcomes have increasingly become one way to articulate this curriculum. We expect students to know and be able to do a set of tasks at various points in their schooling careers. This list of learning expectations is then translated into learning materials, such as textbooks, which may be accompanied by teachers' manuals that help both teachers and students meet the expectations. Some communities refer to these learning expectations as "curricular aims," "common curricular goals," "standards," and "benchmarks."

The underlying logic of curricular aims or approved standard curriculum, whether standards based or not, is that if a student learns this content, then the student is likely to be able to use it to become an active, contributing member of the community. Put another way, our communities need children, youth, and adults who have learned and can use these bits of information and demonstrate these skills.

Historically, this logic has served teachers and students reasonably well. Many students have learned much of what is contained in the official curriculum and textbooks—at least momentarily—and most do go on to construct active, contributing lives. We find ourselves troubled today, however, by the students who don't seem to fit into a prescribed curriculum, as well as by adults who report that they "never learned anything useful in school." Too many students promptly forget much of what they learned as they pursue their own interests and lives, cleanly decoupling school learning from life. School learning becomes a kind of job that must occupy the days of our children and youth, but has little relevance to the *real* learning that supports how they live their lives. Part of our purpose in this book is to make school learning more meaningful *life* learning.

The purpose of schooling is *not* to make every child learn everything that is in the official curriculum. It is to help students acquire the competence to be active, valued members of their communities. If learning all, or even most, of the official curriculum accomplishes this purpose, so much the better. But if learning the official curriculum does not seem to result in students' ability to use their learning, teachers must make different curricular decisions.

As our society changes from an industrial structure to one reliant on information technology, the logic of an official curriculum becomes less useful. Our emerging society is making far different demands. A schooling in facts and skills will be less useful than one that prepares adults to creatively seek out information, create new information, and respond to the problems and purposes of each day.

Standards and other forms of official curricula are, and will remain, useful to teachers as long as they are periodically reviewed and revised by our communities. We should remember, however, that such standards or shared learning aims

are meant to guide how teachers work with learners toward those goals. By themselves, official curriculum standards, even when learned, cannot ensure that learners will be successful in achieving the goals set for them.

Curriculum as Decision Making

Given the nature of the official curriculum and the important purposes of schooling for children and youth, it is most powerful and effective if teachers think of curriculum as first and foremost about teacher decision making. Teachers must first decide how well the official curriculum or achievement standards are working to achieve educational outcomes for each student. They must then decide how to tweak official curriculum activities to incorporate other learning tasks so that individually tailored and effective learning experiences will occur for every student. Many teachers do this tweaking automatically, following some kind of instinct, but don't typically take the time either beforehand or afterward to reflect about why they are making these decisions.

In this chapter, we show how teachers can make those sorts of curricular plans and decisions more deliberately by using a deeper understanding of every student's needs and abilities. We begin by describing three broad types of curricular decision making that teachers use repeatedly. Examples from Ms. Clark's class will probably look familiar.

Three Decision-Making Situations

Teachers encounter three kinds of decision-making situations, based on the unique ways their students learn and use their learning. The kinds of curricular decisions teachers may need to make are slightly different for each one, but all students are likely to benefit, making their learning more productive and meaningful.

Enriching the Curriculum

Some students seem to float through whatever teachers are teaching, learning with apparent ease and interest at least most of the time. They generally do well enough on measures of acquisition and achievement. They function well in their lives outside school and as members of their peer group. These are the easy situations that make a teacher's job both comfortable and satisfying. But teachers are not always sure if such students remember any of the learning or if they just operate outside school on the basis of what they learn there instead of in school. Teachers may also wonder about their inability to excite any real passion about learning for some students. The students learn what is taught, and they meet criteria—they are the "good citizens." But teachers are concerned about transmitting their passion for learning to their students.

We think such students need teachers to find ways to enrich the curriculum for them, to help them identify and get excited about their learning and its usefulness in their lives. If there is a "goodness of fit" between what students are learning in school and the interests and demands of their lives outside school, their learning will be more meaningful and sensible to them. This kind of identification with what they are learning is the real stuff of both learning motivation and passion for learning. They might also learn more deeply. Most students need teachers to make enrichment decisions at least part of the time, as illustrated by the case of Samuel.

Samuel is an example of a student who generally finishes his assignments well ahead of the class. Often, Ms. Clark will announce to the class that Samuel is available to help and that he doesn't mind circling around the room. Most kids are receptive, and the teacher appreciates the support. But she questions if placing him in this role is fair and if it enhances his learning. Certainly it helps his social interaction with his peers. The class easily respects him as smart.

One day, Samuel had finished a guided reading activity on early civilizations 30 minutes ahead of everyone else. With his pleasant smile, he asked, "What shall I do now?" The rest of the class had the task in hand, and the teacher sensed that asking him to help others was avoiding the real issue. Samuel was entitled to a challenge. He needed to puzzle over tasks or activities the way his classmates did. She knew she was not meeting his needs. Grasping for an idea, she asked Samuel if he wanted to build a Sumerian water clock from some old directions she had found. His eyes lighted up and off he went. Since then, Samuel still helps Eli, Josh, and even Amanda, but at other times, the teacher offers Samuel—for his own learning—project ideas that she will never get around to using with the whole class.

Enhancing the Curriculum

There are students who may draw a teacher's special attention. It's not that they are not learning—it's that they learn so quickly that they have time to fool around and distract others. Such students may become bored and frustrated because they feel they waste time waiting for others, and they may gradually lose all interest. They drop out and stop trying. Their ability to meet the standards of achievement that teachers and schools have set quickly diminishes.

Other students may struggle with their learning. They take longer to figure something out and sometimes despair of ever succeeding. Some learning is more drudgery than discovery. Students feel little passion and, over time, little interest in learning. Struggling students may try to handle their frustration by making even less effort, arguing that they don't need to learn what teachers ask of them to be successful in their lives. Once a student has made this kind of decision to devalue school learning, it can be almost impossible to change the student's mind.

Both bored and struggling students need teachers to enhance the curriculum to respond not just to their abilities, but also to their learning styles, preferences, personal interests, and intelligences. Children may struggle, for example, because they are active, inductive learners who find rote, repetitive, deductive learning incomprehensible and boring. Facile learners often need more areas to learn and explore that build

upon their interests and preferred ways of learning so that they can make learning alive in their lives.

All learners have various intelligences, or ways of receiving and expressing their knowledge. These intelligences can serve as a powerful springboard for creative curricular decision making and instructional planning. Howard Gardner (1993), the leading multiple intelligences theorist, has identified eight so far, and other educators, such as Goleman (1995), are defining more. Here are some of them:

- Kinesthetic intelligence.
- Musical intelligence.
- Logical-mathematical intelligence.
- Linguistic intelligence.
- Interpersonal intelligence.
- Intrapersonal intelligence.
- Spatial intelligence.
- Naturalistic intelligence.
- Emotional intelligence.

All learners, including those with significantly different abilities, cultural backgrounds, and family lives, have both strengths and needs in each of these areas. Teachers need to draw upon and strengthen *all* of a student's intelligences. Students who discover new ways to apply and build on the range of skills that they already possess develop true self-esteem. Such meaningful experiences can sustain them during more challenging learning activities.

There are many ways to enhance the curriculum to respond to a student's intelligences, learning styles, and learning preferences. The demands of the task can be changed (e.g., give more or fewer examples, read more or fewer pages or books). Teachers might change the focus of the task. An example might be allowing students to learn a curricular goal—such as learn basic probability—by studying basketball teams and player statistics. Another example might be to learn about adjectives and adverbs by being the notetaker for a science experiment. Working on a curricular goal can occur within the context of an activity or lesson that might focus on a different curricular topic.

Teachers can enhance the options of what students produce. For one student, the assignment to write about his family might mean exploring his family tree and writing about distant relatives and the language they spoke in the old country. For another student, it might mean writing about her family's interest in hiking through the mountain forests, an interest the student passionately shares with her family. It might mean drawing, writing a song, or videotaping a play instead of actually writing out the assignment. In the end, the students will learn the official curricular aims, but their different ways of acquiring and using the knowledge are what make the curriculum useful in building the students' competence and value as members of their community.

Ms. Clark and her student Brandon both learned from the following experience. Brandon is constantly doodling or drawing when expected to work independently. During a reading fluency activity, which required him to choose a story, listen to a tape, reread the passage to the teacher, then produce a written retell, he consis-

tently chose bug stories. After Brandon had practiced his reading, the teacher was later exasperated to see him drawing again instead of working on his writing assignment. She looked at his paper and discovered an intricate picture map depicting each aspect of the original story. He glanced at her sheepishly as she stood beside him. She encouraged him to tell her about his drawing. He explained the life cycle of a moth in detail. She asked him to complete the drawing, giving him permission to retell his selections in the picture map format, which he is most comfortable with. His confidence in his ability to retell his selections soared. It had taken her a moment to realize that Brandon was exhibiting a benchmark skill in his preferred alternative style.

Overlapping and Embedding the Curriculum

Teachers may have students whose abilities make it impossible for them to learn in some areas. Barriers to learning can be physical; medical; emotional; or a reflection of a student's history, culture, or personality. In these types of situations, teachers have to be guided directly by the schooling outcomes and the student's strengths to align the student's learning needs more closely with the official curriculum. Of course, a number of these students can learn many, even all, parts of the official curriculum, especially when teachers are creative and flexible. Others, like Susannah in the following narrative, will work on communication objectives, which are tied to the state benchmarks for communication, during the class's literacy learning activities that are aligned with another part of the official curriculum.

Using the official curriculum as the only teaching reference may not allow teachers to be as confident that their teaching is helping a student become a more active and contributing member of the community. Teachers must select those parts of the curriculum that *directly* build students' competence in the activities of real life, both inside and outside school.

Susannah's teachers weren't sure if Susannah would be able to participate in a 6th grade literature circle. Literature circles require five students to choose a book, plan the reading calendar, set up a schedule for group members to take a role for participation within the group, and discuss the book. They later answer questions about the book during a group presentation. The roles include discussion director, literary luminary, illustrator, connector, and summarizer. Some teachers add other roles.

Ms. Jackson, the speech-language specialist, was focusing on Susannah's communication goals: to articulate and comprehend functional vocabulary and to follow directions. Ms. Clark offered the class a choice of six books to vote on. Susannah voted for *Woodsong* because she liked the picture of dogs on the cover.

Groups began to form, and Susannah joined a group with four other students interested in *Woodsong*. Ms. Jackson monitored the group as the students chose roles. Susannah began with the role of Word Wizard, which required her to choose vocabulary words from the book's first chapter. The speech-language specialist, Ms. Jackson, helped Susannah choose words contain-

ing sounds that they were practicing. Susannah wrote her word list. The group went to the two comfortable couches in the back of the room to listen to the first chapter on tape as they followed along in their books. To the teachers' delight, Susannah participated in the group activity while also working on her communication goals. For Susannah, curricular decisions involved finding ways to embed or overlap her communication objectives in activities like literature circles in which other students' objectives are focused more on reading.

* * *

In the following chapters, we present strategies to help teachers make these three kinds of curricular decisions and assess their students' outcomes from a more individual and personalized perspective. Here is what we present:

• Ways to get to know your students' and their families' interests and learning priorities more personally, deeply, and quickly than is often typical. Knowing students well helps teachers feel confident that students understand the relevancy of what they are learning to their real-life activities. (See Chapters 2 and 3.)
• Examples of how to build curriculum plans using an activity-based assessment. (See Chapters 3 and 4.)
• Processes and tools to identify, discuss, and document student learning gains that are seen in the classroom but don't necessarily appear in state benchmark exams. Such gains are valuable to both the student and the student's family.

(See Chapters 5 and 6.)

• Strategies to elicit validating information from families on how their children are using their new learning and skills in the community activities that they identified earlier as high priority. (See Chapter 3.)

References

Gardner, H. (1993). *Multiple intelligences: The theory in practice.* New York: BasicBooks.

Goleman, D. (1995). *Emotional intelligence.* New York: Bantam Books.

For Further Reading

If you are interested in learning more about differentiated instruction, you may want to take a look at the work of Tomlinson (1996, 1997a, 1997b, 1999). The book edited by Pugach and Warger (1996) and the book edited by Falvey (1995) discuss the history of general and special education reforms and how the two movements can unite through curriculum design. The books by Armstrong (1994a, 1994b, 1998) use Gardner's theory of multiple intelligences to discuss the inner gifts and genius in all students, especially students labeled with disabilities. The resources by Chard (1998a, 1998b) offer educators an introduction to and numerous examples of the "project approach."

Armstrong, T. (1994a). Multiple intelligences: Seven ways to approach curriculum. *Educational Leadership,* 52(3), 26–28.

Armstrong, T. (1994b). *Multiple intelligences in the classroom.* Alexandria, VA: Association for Supervision and Curriculum Development.

Armstrong, T. (1998). *Awakening genius in the classroom.* Alexandria, VA: Association for Supervision and Curriculum Development.

Chard, S. C. (1998a). *The project approach: Developing the basic framework: Practical guide 1.* New York: Scholastic.

Chard, S. C. (1998b). *The project approach: Developing curriculum with children: Practical guide 2.* New York: Scholastic.

Falvey, M. A. (Ed.). (1995). *Inclusive and heterogeneous schooling: Assessment, curriculum, and instruction.* Baltimore: Paul H. Brookes Publishing.

Pugach, M. C., & Warger, C. L. (Eds.). (1996). *Curriculum trends, special education, and reform: Refocusing the conversation.* New York: Teachers College Press.

Tomlinson, C. A. (Developer). (1996). *Differentiating instruction for mixed-ability classrooms: An ASCD professional inquiry kit.* Alexandria, VA: Association for Supervision and Curriculum Development.

Tomlinson, C. A. (Educational Consultant). (1997a). *Differentiating instruction. tape 1: Creating multiple paths for learning with facilitator's guide* [Videotape]. Alexandria, VA: Association for Supervision and Curriculum Development.

Tomlinson, C. A. (Educational Consultant). (1997b). *Differentiating instruction. Tape 2: Instructional and management strategies* [Videotape]. Alexandria, VA: Association for Supervision and Curriculum Development.

Tomlinson, C. A. (1999). *The differentiated classroom: Responding to the needs of all learners.* Alexandria, VA: Association for Supervision and Curriculum Development.

Gathering Information About Your Students

Even students with similar learning styles benefit when instruction is tailored to their learning preferences and personal interests. This chapter describes two strategies to help discover these preferences and interests. One strategy focuses on how students use their learning outside school; teachers might use it to complete meaningful and comprehensive assessments so that they can design learning activities and objectives for each student. The other strategy helps teachers collect information about students' learning histories, so that one teacher's efforts can begin where other teachers have left off.

Activity-Based Assessment (ABA): Figuring Out Who Students Are

Teachers typically have a variety of official achievement information about their students. In fact, most schools seem to excel at collecting information about how each student compares to all the other students. Even detailed information may be available about how far a student has progressed through some curricular content or toward a set of standards.

To help them learn more about students' learning styles, preferences, and intelligences, teachers are also beginning to use inventories. The need to learn more is driven by the fact that teachers cannot always depend exclusively upon the official curriculum to achieve desired schooling outcomes for all their students. They must instead look to the activities and patterns of the lives students are leading as an important curricular source, and then *overlap and embed* real-life learning goals into the curriculum. The approach of examining students' lives—activities they enjoy or are even passionate about and activities they would like to explore—to inform curriculum and teaching design is called activity-based assessment (ABA). Here we offer a specific strategy for doing activity-based assessment: the Activity-Based Assessment Inventory (the ABA Inventory). The inventory consists of lists of activities that children and youth of different ages typically do. When teachers use the ABA Inventory, they learn what students and their families value about learning and what students might want schools to help them accomplish in their lives.

The ABA Inventory

The ABA Inventory was first created to help teachers of students with significant cognitive or physical disabilities identify those activities their students most needed to learn and were most interested in learning about. The teachers involved in the work that led to this book expanded its use to help them learn more about *all* their students. Here is what they wanted to learn:

• Each student's competence to participate in the day-to-day activities typical of their age group.
• Which of these day-to-day activities students themselves want to learn more about or perform better.
• Which of these activities students' family and friends identify as priorities for learning and participation.

Such information can be used to make appropriate enrichment, enhancement, or overlapping decisions about curriculum for each student when needed.

The inventory can help students with differing needs, such as those nearing the end of their schooling or who have reached such a level of frustration with school that a whole new approach is called for. Students approaching graduation might use the ABA Inventory to identify what they still need to learn to make a successful transition to work or college. Other students who benefit include those with significant disabilities and those who have moved often from school to school, rarely experiencing the coherence of an entire year's learning. Teachers may want to use only a part of the assessment because only one part of a student's learning is challenging. For example, students who are shy and socially uncomfortable may benefit from an in-depth analysis of their interests and abilities about recreation and leisure activities.

The ABA Inventory has two parts: the ABA Age-Appropriate Activity Lists and the ABA Summary. We discuss each part and suggest ways to use them.

ABA Age-Appropriate Activity Lists

Schooling should help every student be an active, contributing member of a community now, not at some time in the distant future. *The age-appropriate activity lists represent the real-life curriculum that the official curriculum seeks to influence.*

Developed by interviewing students, parents, and teachers about what children and youth actually *do* in their lives outside school, the lists are organized into four age groups (ages 5–8, 9–12, 13–15, and 16+) and activities that involve "caring for self, friends, and family," "contributing to community," and "enjoying leisure and recreation." Each age group has a five-page activity list.[1] Figure 2.1 shows the range and diversity of activities included on the lists by comparing three types of activities and two age groupings.

The ABA Inventory was designed to help structure a conversation with a student and the student's family and friends. Figure 2.2 outlines five steps to guide teachers during this interview. Some teachers like to sit between the student and others so all can see the activity list.

These questions focus on learning about the student's abilities, interests, and priorities for learning and change. Interesting or potentially useful information can be noted in the spaces on the list. Some teachers are tempted to omit items because they think that the student can't do them or isn't interested in them. These items, however, may turn out to be the ones the family is most interested in.

Figure 2.3, on page 29, shows how Ms. Clark used one page of the inventory's activity list for Josh's age group (9–12) to record her interview with Josh. We can see Josh's interests and the activities he would like to do more. He some-

times has trouble staying on task, so Ms. Clark would like to offer him opportunities to do work that holds his attention and that he enjoys. She thought that completing the ABA Inventory with him would help her better tailor his assignments to his interests.

After the information is recorded on the activity list, the list can be saved in the student's cumulative file. As a record of the student's competence and growth, it will provide valuable information for others as well as a useful contrast with the more deficit-oriented information typically found in official files. Ms. Clark reports that several teachers who inherited her students have let her know that the ABA Inventory information was helpful.

The ABA Summary

Once the interview is completed, the one-page ABA Summary is a helpful way to consolidate what has been learned. Figure 2.4, on page 30, shows a filled-out example for Josh. When it's time to make curricular decisions, Ms. Clark has found that the ABA Summary helps bring the conversations back to mind and precludes the need for flipping through all the inventory pages. She routinely uses the summary for long-term curriculum planning. The summary can also be a useful way to share the interview easily with other teachers who together plan curriculum and teaching. In fact, Ms. Clark shares it with special education staff for IEP planning to help them tie IEP goals more closely to a student's interests.

---

[1] The complete five-page ABA Inventory for each age group is available at http://www.edc.org/urban.

2.1	Activities from the ABA Age-Appropriate Activity Lists		

Age Group	TYPE OF ACTIVITY		
	Caring for Self, Family, and Friends	**Contributing to Community**	**Enjoying Leisure and Recreation**
5–8	Being a friend. Family membership. Personal care. Personal business.	School membership and commitments (e.g., school clubs and groups). Community membership and commitments (e.g., community clubs and groups).	Media. Exercise and fitness. Events. Games, crafts, and hobbies.
16+	Being a friend. Family membership. Personal care. Personal business.	After school, weekend, and vacation jobs. Categories: Arts and communication. Business management. Health services. Human resources. Industrial and engineering systems. Natural resource systems. Miscellaneous.	Media. Exercise and fitness. Events. Games, crafts, and hobbies.

Wait—Teachers Can't Spend So Much Time with Every Student!

We realize that teachers don't have time to interview all their students. Individual interviews should be conducted only with the few students who require the most curriculum tailoring. For other students, a whole-group approach to activity-based assessment still results in valuable individual information. Activity-based assessment can be used in several ways with whole groups. We offer three.

All Students Complete the Age-Appropriate List

With middle or high school students, an age-appropriate activity list can be handed out to the entire class. Students fill out the list, identifying those activities they most like to do with a star and those they think they need to do or would like to do better with a check. The lists could even be creatively formatted into other graphics with the help of a computer.

All Students Complete a Questionnaire or Written Interview

Another approach is to use the lists to develop a questionnaire or written interview in which students write down or talk about preferred activities without using the lists as a source. The student questionnaire shown in Figure 2.5, on page 31, was created by two teachers; Ms. Clark used it to learn about Becky's interests.

All Students and Families Complete the Age-Appropriate List

The appropriate activity list could also be sent home with students with a cover letter suggesting that the parents and student review it together. They might summarize their home discussion by making a list of several activities they would like to focus on during the course of the year. Figure 2.6, on page 32, provides a sample cover letter that Ms. Clark sent to parents

---

2.2	Guide to Using the ABA Age-Appropriate Activity Lists

1. Select the activity list that matches your students' age.

2. Make copies of the activity list for all students in your class. Consider giving the list to parents before you meet so they can become familiar with it and review it with their children.

3. Schedule a time (about 1½ hours) to meet with the student, the student's parents, and any siblings who the student or parents think might have useful information or ideas.

4. Make notes on the activity list as the interview proceeds.

5. Keep the interview positive. You're trying to learn about the student's abilities, interests, and preferences so you can make better curricular decisions.

Excerpt from a Student's ABA Inventory

AGES 9–12

ENJOYING LEISURE AND RECREATION
(continued)

Student Name: *Josh Finley*
Date: *September 20, 2000*

Teachers: Ask students these questions for each activity: How do you do this? When? Where? Is this something you want to change? Feel free to check, circle, or underline. Make notes everywhere!

EVENTS . . . .

☞ 7. COMMUNITY
▲ Attending or participating in (fairs?)
▲ Attending (festivals,) (exhibits,) and (museums:) *Eugene and Orange County in California*
▲ Attending and participating in community events for kids and families: *Yes, especially holidays*

☞ 8. ENTERTAINMENT
▲ Attending movies: *Yes*
▲ Attending events such as car rallies, pet shows, races, and air shows: *No*
▲ Visiting the zoo, planetarium, and (aquarium:) *Sea World*

☞ 9. CULTURAL
▲ Attending art shows and museums: *Yes   Historical*
▲ Attending or participating in cultural performances such as concerts, plays, and dances: *No*

Which ones do you want to begin doing or do more?

Go to dances and concerts

☞ 10. SPORTS
▲ Attending or participating in sports events: *Yes, Mighty Ducks hockey*

☞ 11. TRAVEL
▲ Summer camps: *Vacations in Coos Bay*

GAMES, HOBBIES, & CRAFTS . . . .

☞ 12. PLAYING GAMES
▲ Board games: *Uno, Battleship, Connect 4*
▲ Video and computer games: *Yes   Sim City*
▲ Toys (e.g., Lego's or dolls):

☞ 13. CREATING ART
▲ Drawing and painting: *Yes*
▲ Calligraphy: *No*
▲ Ceramics: *Yes*
▲ Woodwork or metalwork: *Yes*
▲ Jewelry making:
▲ Stained glass: *No*
▲ Origami:

☞ 14. CREATING NEEDLE CRAFTS
▲ Sewing: *No*
▲ Knitting: *No*
▲ Weaving: *No*
▲ Crocheting: *No*
▲ Leatherwork: *No*

☞ 15. COLLECTING
▲ Coins: *Yes*
▲ Stamps: *No*
▲ Stickers:
▲ Rocks: *Yes*
▲ Trading cards: *Yes, collecting Pokemon* ☆

☞ 16. PHOTOGRAPHY
▲ Using a camera: *No*
▲ Putting in a photo album: *No*

☞ 17. CONSTRUCTING OR PLAYING WITH
▲ Models: *Yes*
▲ Kites: *Yes*
▲ Puzzles: *Yes*

☞ 18. MUSIC
▲ Singing: *Yes*
▲ Playing an instrument: *Yes, drums*

☞ 19. SCIENCE: *Yes*

☞ 20. LANGUAGES: *No*

Which ones do you want to begin doing or do more?

Ceramics
Metalwork
Music—band

2.4	Example of a Student's ABA Summary

ABA Individual Student Summary

Student Name: *Josh Finley*
Discussion Participants: *Rachel and Ken Finley*
Interviewer: *Ms. Clark*
Date: *September 20, 2000*

✔	Initial ABA Inventory
☐	Year 2 update
☐	Year 3 update

General Picture of Student's Interests and Participation	Ideas, Priorities, and Preferences
Caring for self, friends, and family *Being a friend: Good social skills.* *Family membership: Has chores, but very disorganized.* *Personal care: Good, overall self-management.* *Personal business: Takes care of things as needed, but often gets distracted and off task.*	*Independent, likes to try things on own.* *Likes to manage own schedule.* *Group "social director"—very outgoing; needs to have chances to be leader and follower; part of the team.* *Home chores expanding; could include pet care and car washing.*
Contributing to community *School membership and commitments: Has class jobs; has trouble following directions.* *Community membership and commitments: Involved in church group and club.* *Jobs and chores: Does some weeding and gardening; car washing.*	*Reading group—share readings and reports.* *Would like to learn tennis "for real." Check for old racquets and balls; also dancing.* *PE dance unit.* *Metal—explore.* *Has interest in ceramics; work with clay in class.*
Enjoying leisure and recreation *Media: Good reading skills; reads for pleasure.* *Exercise and fitness: Participates in lots of outdoor recreation.* *Events: Has opportunity to do holiday activities with family and visit coast.* *Games, crafts, and hobbies: Music; loves to drum.*	*Parents not sure about class involvement; likes to be busy helping; make sure to give jobs and roles in class.* *No volunteering yet: likes the idea and maybe partner with younger students in spring.* *Likes to be out and active: learn more about metal shop and band or music opportunities.*

2.5   Example of a Student's Questionnaire

Student Name: **Becky Wilson**   Date: **September 20, 2000**

My pets:

Cat, Claudius

All About Me

Home chores:

1. Dishes
2. Cat care
3. My room
4.
5.

Things that make me laugh:

1. Far Side
2. The Simpsons
3. My dad
4.

Hobbies and sports:

1. Basketball
2. Reading
3. Clarinet
4.

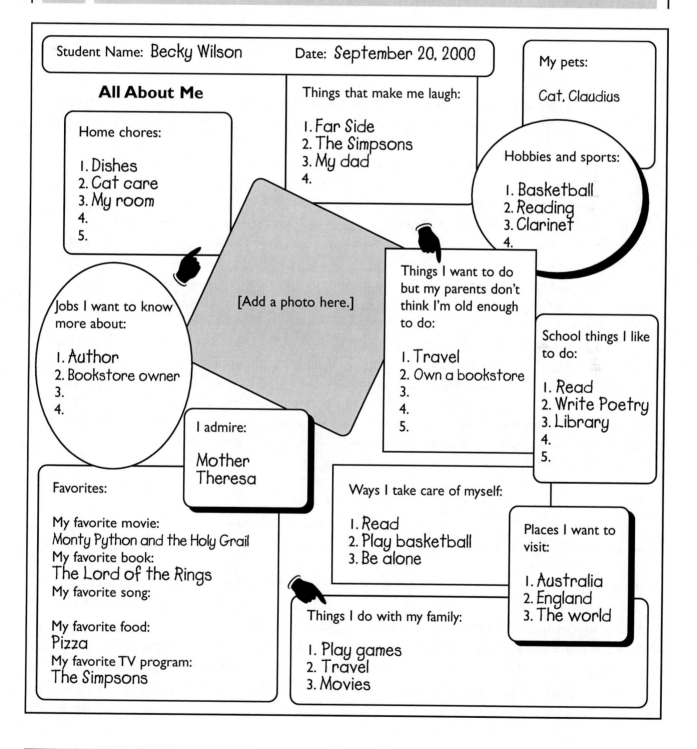

[Add a photo here.]

Jobs I want to know more about:

1. Author
2. Bookstore owner
3.
4.

Things I want to do but my parents don't think I'm old enough to do:

1. Travel
2. Own a bookstore
3.
4.
5.

School things I like to do:

1. Read
2. Write Poetry
3. Library
4.
5.

I admire:

Mother Theresa

Favorites:

My favorite movie:
Monty Python and the Holy Grail
My favorite book:
The Lord of the Rings
My favorite song:

My favorite food:
Pizza
My favorite TV program:
The Simpsons

Ways I take care of myself:

1. Read
2. Play basketball
3. Be alone

Places I want to visit:

1. Australia
2. England
3. The world

Things I do with my family:

1. Play games
2. Travel
3. Movies

| 2.6 | Sample Cover Letter to Accompany an Age-Appropriate Activity List |

Dear _____,

The year seems off to its usual hectic start! I will try to keep you informed of important events and activities as each week and month pass, but this letter is to first solicit some important information from you and _____.

I want to make sure that the curriculum and learning activities we do this year are useful and sensible for _____. I am especially interested in making sure that whatever _____ learns is interesting and seems to have some usefulness in _____'s life outside school.

Attached is a list of activities that children _____'s age typically do. Please sit down with _____ and talk about which of these activities _____ does well enough and which _____ and you might want to get better at.

Of course, I can't promise that I will be able to work directly on all these activities, but knowing about the interests and preferences of you and _____ will help me tailor assignments and activities to try to incorporate these interests.

I have scheduled a parents' meeting for October 12 at 7:00 p.m. It will last about an hour and a half. I've invited all the parents of my students to attend so that we can discuss the list. Please try to select three to five activities that are especially important to you and _____. Of course, you can also write me a note or call me at_____ if you cannot attend this meeting or if you prefer meeting individually. I am hoping that getting the parents together will help identify ways in which we can all work together to make this year an especially successful and productive one for _____.

Feel free to call or write me if you have questions or just want to talk things over.

Regards,
Ms. Clark

---

explaining the list.

As the figure shows, the letter includes an invitation to parents to attend a meeting to talk about curriculum and learning activities for the coming year. Teachers have used this approach successfully; Chapter 3 provides an extended example of one teacher's experience in her kindergarten class. We describe here part of one such meeting among Ms. Clark and some of her students' parents.

Jamie's aunt didn't say much for the first 15 or 20 minutes of the meeting. She seemed shy, sitting on the edge of the group and clasping her hands in her lap as if she were a little uncomfortable being back in a school.

Susannah's mother began talking about her desire for Susannah to do more with friends after school. She worried about Susannah being at home alone watching TV with her brother until her mother arrived home from work. She asked if Ms. Clark might help the students plan some after-school activities with each other once in a while.

Jamie's aunt seemed to gather her courage, nervously cleared her throat, and said she was worried about Jamie not having many friends and being so sullen and isolated. She had recently received custody of him, but did not seem sure about how to support Jamie's pre-adolescent social life.

Bill's mother spoke up, offering to make sure Jamie was invited to Bill's upcoming birthday party. Two other parents made similar offers. Josh's dad commented that Josh often mentioned Jamie in his reports about the school day's events and seemed to like him. He offered to encourage Josh to invite Jamie over for videos and popcorn some evening soon.

After the meeting, Ms. Clark completed an ABA Summary for Jamie and Susannah. She could also have used an ABA whole-class summary page to make notes on all students in the class instead of making a separate summary for each student. A whole-class summary is often a more efficient way for many teachers to keep this information at hand when planning curriculum events and lessons. In subsequent chapters, information from Jamie's and Susannah's summaries appear in curriculum and teaching plans.

The History/Transition Information Profile

Every fall in U.S. schools, many teachers get a new group of students, and most students get a new teacher. Some schools are experimenting with "step-ups," in which a teacher follows her class to the next grade, and with mixed-age groupings that allow students to stay with the same teacher for several years. This practice has been common in other countries, where teachers follow their students, sometimes through elementary and middle school. For most teachers, however, a new group of students arrives each September.

Teachers may know a little about some of their new students from seeing them around the school or, in some cases, from hearing previous teachers talk about them in the teachers' lounge or during meetings. Too often, though, teachers don't know much about their new group of students and have to start from scratch getting to know each one. Teachers may go through a whole year and still feel that they have never gotten to know a number of their students.

Not really getting to know their students before the students move on can be frustrating for teachers. They realize that if they do get to know students well, they are more likely to be able to tailor the learning so that it is interesting and more useful. Such knowledge often results in higher overall achievement. What may be even more troublesome is that teachers sometimes teach students for a whole year with only the information they pick up in the halls and teachers' lounge, missing an opportunity to design the more personalized learning that knowing the students better would permit.

Although the ABA Inventory assists the process of learning who students are, it does not provide teachers with an educational history of their students. What have past teachers learned about students' preferred learning styles? What are their special gifts of intelligence? What supports do they need to manage school and learning well? What kinds of curricular materials and approaches have been tried? Which worked and which didn't?

Of course, for some students, this kind of information is less critical, or it becomes obvious within a few days. For a sizable portion of the class, however, a teacher could spend the fall covering old ground. The History/Transition Information Profile was created to help obtain this information sooner rather than later. Figure 2.7 is a synopsis of the three-page profile (available at http://www.edc.org/urban). Figure 2.8 on page 36, shows how Ms. Clark completed one of the three pages for Tasha.

Responsibility for filling out the profile varies. If a school is well organized as collaborating faculty, a system could be developed in which *sending* teachers fill out the profile for students they think might be difficult to learn about quickly. If a school is not organized in this way, teachers of incoming students could ask the sending teachers to complete the profile with the child's parents before the end of the school year. They could also use the form as an interview guide after the student has moved on to the next teacher. The new teacher can use the transition profile to gather information from both the previous teacher and the student's parents. Some teachers find the profile especially helpful when students move to a new school.

In Grandview's school district, all 5th grade teachers complete a shorter, condensed transition overview for students moving to the middle school. Figure 2.9, on page 37, shows Tasha's.

It is important not to leave out the student's parents when gathering information. Although one year can generate much valuable information to pass on to a new teacher, that information comes from a classroom context that might be different from the new classroom. We have found that parents are typically better than teachers at anticipating how their child will react to a new classroom environment. Parents' information might be crucial to the peacefulness and productivity of the first weeks of the new year and serve as a basis for curricular decisions throughout the year.

* * *

Taking students' and families' perspectives into account is key to creating an effective, flexible curriculum and genuinely reinvented schools. The next chapter provides additional ideas, strategies, and tools to help use this information about students in both whole-class and individual student planning.

2.7	Synopsis of the Student History/Transition Information Profile		

Topics for Grouping Student's Abilities, Issues, and Needs	From Teacher's Perspective	From Family's Perspective	Where to Find More Information
Reading Writing Schedule use/time telling Calendar Numbers/math Money Independent work Group work Homework			
Health and safety Communication Mobility Manipulation Vision/hearing Personal care Equipment			
Self-management/behavior Friends/relationships Learning style/preferences Activity level preferences Social image/self-esteem Other home information Other school information Other community information			

2.8	Excerpt from a Student's History/Transition Information Profile

Student Name: *Tasha Moro*   Date: *September 20, 2000*

Student's Abilities, Issues, and Needs	From Teacher's Perspective	From Family's Perspective	Where to Find More Information
Health and Safety: Has had several surgeries on her back and legs		Mom will keep school updated on surgeries.	Medical file with school nurse.
Communication: Expressive. Stutters while reading and in conversation Receptive: Great comprehension	Tasha loves to sing and has been involved with choir. Enjoys reciting poetry. Her stuttering is greatly decreased when singing, reciting, or performing. Swimming for adaptive P.E. five times a week. Check with OT or PT. OT to monitor weekly. PT to monitor monthly.	Mom sings professionally. She is supportive of choir and music. Enjoys recreational swimming as family activity. Mom will keep school updated on needs.	Speech file with SLP. With OT or PT.
Mobility: Limited ability to walk; does not need cane or crutches at this time; OT to monitor leg braces			
Manipulation: Good			
Vision/hearing: Good			
Personal care (meal time, grooming, and hygiene): Needs help dressing after swimming; good grooming and hygiene			
Equipment: Cane or crutches at times; leg braces			

Note: OT = occupational therapist; PT = physical therapist; SLP = speech-language professional.

2.9	Example of a Student's Transition Overview

Student Name: *Tasha Moro*   School: *Wasilla Elementary*
Sending Teacher: *Ms. Barnes*   Date: *June 30, 1999*

Briefly, a few things you might like to know about: *Tasha Moro*

Student is especially good at . . .
- *Math*
- *Singing*
- *Poetry*
- *Reading*
- *Writing*

Things that have worked well for the student are . . .
- *Tons of encouragement*
- *Chorale reading*
- *Rhythmic activities to pace oral reading*
- *Giving her alternative formats for oral presentations*
- *Letting her sing*

Things you need to be on top of quickly include . . .
- *Tasha has a moderate speech dysfluency (stuttering) that is exacerbated by anxiety and frustration.*

Things that didn't work well for us were . . .
- *Pressure*
- *Putting her on the spot without prior warning*

Comments:
- *Very bright—likes to help or mentor other students*
- *Is seen by an occupational therapist or a physical therapist*

For Further Reading

Sometimes it's helpful to step back a moment to reexamine our own sense of the purpose of education. Fishman and McCarthy (1998) revisit some of Dewey's (1938) ideas, and if you haven't read his work in awhile, it's worth exploring how timeless many of his ideas are. Noddings (1992) also reminds us to think first and foremost about the children we work with. We think the stories of change by Berres, Ferguson, Knoblock, and Woods (1996); Meier (1995); and Rose (1995) —with examples from schools, classrooms, teachers, and students—can be helpful in considering issues in your own district.

We've also included some readings by Middlebrooks (1998); Muller, Katz, and Dance (1999); Scheurich (1998); and Schultz (1999). They focus on the issues and unique challenges that urban schools and districts face.

A selection of writings covers a range of issues in the area of disability, including attitudes about disability and creating curriculum and environments that support and sustain youth with serious emotional disturbances and significant cognitive disabilities: Miller and Sammons (1999); Sinclair, Christenson, Evelo, and Hurley (1998); Tam and Gardner (1997); and Vandercook, Medwetz, Montie, Taylor, and Scaletta (1997).

The book by Burt, Resnick, and Novick (1998) explores the challenges involved in creating and sustaining supportive communities for at-risk youth.

Berres, M. S., Ferguson, D. L., Knoblock, P., & Woods, C. (Eds.). (1996). *Creating tomorrow's schools today: Stories of inclusion, change, and renewal.* New York: Teachers College Press.

Burt, M. R., Resnick, G., & Novick, E. R. (1998). *Building supportive communities for at-risk adolescents: It takes more than services.* Washington, DC: American Psychological Association.

Dewey, J. (1938). *Experience and education.* New York: Macmillan Publishing Company.

Fishman, S. M., & McCarthy, L. (1998). *John Dewey and the challenge of classroom practice.* New York: Teachers College Press.

Meier, D. (1995). *The power of their ideas: Lessons for America from a small school in Harlem.* Boston, MA: Beacon Press.

Middlebrooks, S. (1998). *Getting to know city kids: Understanding their thinking, imagining, and socializing.* New York: Teachers College Press.

Miller, N. B., & Sammons, C. C. (1999). *Everybody's different: Understanding and changing our reactions to disabilities.* Baltimore: Paul H. Brookes Publishing.

Muller, C., Katz, S. R., & Dance, L. J. (1999). Investing in teaching and learning: Dynamics of the teacher-student relationship from each actor's perspective. *Urban Education, 34*(3), 292–337.

Noddings, N. (1992). *The challenge to care in schools.* New York: Teachers College Press.

Rose, M. (1995). *Possible lives: The promise of public education in America.* New York: Houghton Mifflin.

Scheurich, J. J. (1998). Highly successful and loving public elementary schools populated mainly by low-SES children of color: Core beliefs and cultural characteristics. *Urban Education, 33*(4), 451–491.

Schultz, K. (1999). Identity narratives: Stories from the lives of urban adolescent females. *The Urban Review, 31*(1), 79–106.

Sinclair, M. F., Christenson, S. L., Evelo, D. L., & Hurley, C. M. (1998). Dropout prevention for youth with disabilities: Efficacy of a sustained school engagement procedure. *Exceptional Children, 65*(1), 7–21.

Tam, B. K. Y., & Gardner, R. (1997). Developing a multicultural and student-centered educational environment for students with serious emotional disturbances. *Multiple Voices for Ethnically Diverse Exceptional Learners, 2*(1), 1–9.

Vandercook, T., Medwetz, L., Montie, J., Taylor, P., & Scaletta, K. (1997). *Lessons for understanding: An elementary school curriculum on perspective taking.* Minneapolis: Institute on Community Integration, University of Minnesota.

Involving Families in Designing Classroom Curriculum

No one could have predicted the effect these activity lists and the work surrounding them would have on my work as a teacher, my relationships with students and their families, and the teaching and learning that would occur during the school year.

—Janet Williams

Earlier chapters discussed strategies for expanding teacher decision making using what teachers know about how students learn generally and what features characterize each year's class specifically. This chapter emphasizes the need for families to be meaningfully involved in that decision-making process. We present one teacher's results of what can happen when families are.[1] Janet Williams's work underscores the belief that understanding what happens when one teacher tests a new idea, implements a new state or district requirement, or tries to meet the challenge of a new student is critical to *really* changing what happens in schools for both teachers and their students.

Williams, an experienced teacher, shared many teachers' interest in wanting to pay more than lip service to "family involvement" in her new kindergarten classroom. But she was concerned about how to implement such an approach efficiently and effectively. In the following narrative, Williams reflects about what happened when she used activity-based assessment as a strategy.

My New Classroom

I had recently moved to a new community and been hired to teach in one of the 15 schools in the

---

[1]A fuller account of Janet Williams's use of activity-based assessment with her class is available in Williams, J., & Ferguson, D. L. (1999). Family involvement in education. *Oregon Schools Study Council Bulletin*. Eugene: University of Oregon. This paper explains not only what Williams and her students' families did, but also how their experiences have begun to spread as other teachers in the school follow their lead. It also describes how Williams, Ferguson, and Guðjónsdóttir worked together to better involve parents in Williams's classroom.

United States recognized as a Basic School by the Carnegie Foundation for the Advancement of Teaching. The first priority of a Basic School is to create a place where everyone comes together to promote learning, including a child's first and most important teachers—their families. As one of two kindergarten teachers, I had the responsibility of welcoming children and their families into our school community and building valued connections between home and school.

In talking with colleagues about family involvement, I learned that most of them valued it. They reported that the most common type of participation included parents helping with miscellaneous clerical work and preparing materials for student use. A few teachers mentioned that parents listened to children read and assisted those who needed extra help. When asked about involving parents in other aspects of education, such as participating in decisions about teaching and learning, many colleagues felt these decisions should be left to the schools. As one colleague explained, "Educators are experts on teaching and learning." When I spoke with parents, though, they expressed an interest in becoming more involved with their children's education, including participating in some of the decision making that would directly affect their children's teaching and learning.

I wanted to develop a genuine collaboration between home and school to bring families closer to the actual teaching and learning in their children's lives. I first encountered the information in this book while it was undergoing revision as a teaching module, and I realized that the ABA Inventory was a concrete way of guiding the conversation I wanted to have with families. Because the inventory could help me learn what parents wanted their children to learn in my classroom, I agreed to help the writing team pilot a new format and an extended application for it.

I first used the inventory with several individual students, meeting with them and their families. I found that the conversations helped me understand more about the children, their families, and their educational goals than all the other assessment information I had from school files. After our discussions, I asked them what they thought about participating in my assessment process. They reported enjoying the experience and felt that other families could benefit from such involvement. They enjoyed most, I think, talking about what their children knew and could do in their daily lives—which is exactly what the process was supposed to elicit. One parent was so enthusiastic about our work together that she offered to help lead other parents in a group meeting to discuss curriculum considerations for their children. Perhaps it was partly this parent's enthusiasm that urged me to try the ABA Inventory with my whole class the following year.

That next year, I held individual orientation meetings before school started. I gave each family the appropriate activity list at these meetings. I explained my purpose for gathering the information: to invite all the families of my students to share information gained from their work with these lists so that we could identify ways we could work together to make the school year especially successful and productive for all the children. I encouraged families to spend time reviewing the lists with their children to identify strengths, interests, and areas of need. I also told parents that the information gathered from their work with these lists would help me design additional learning activities that would be meaningful for their children. I wanted them to know that I was especially interested in making certain that whatever their children learned would be stimulating and useful in life outside school.

At the time, I had no way of knowing the extent to which the lists would help me shape what became the year's curriculum. No one could have predicted the effect these activity lists and the work surrounding them would have on my work as a teacher, my relationships with students and their families, and the teaching and learning that would occur during the school year.

I was a bit apprehensive about my ability to incorporate all the parents' ideas. What if they asked me to address activities that were hard to do in school or did not fit well with the kindergarten curriculum? As I cautioned in a cover letter attached to the lists: "Naturally, I will not be able to work directly on all these things during our time together, but just knowing about the interests and preferences of you and your child will be very helpful as I design lessons and activities."

Family Meetings

Early in the fall, I scheduled one meeting for the parents of the morning class and one for the afternoon class, where I planned to use the age-appropriate activity lists to facilitate a discussion about families' priorities for learning. I hoped we would identify several common interests that I could weave into the kindergarten curriculum.

These first meetings were certainly not what I anticipated. I was hoping to work with a large group of adults, yet only four or five parents attended each meeting, one for each session (morning and afternoon). The parents suggested combining both sessions of kindergarten and meeting again—an idea that turned out to be not only reasonable but also efficient. Still, although the numbers were small, something happened at those first meetings. Was it that someone was interested in knowing what these families valued about their children's learning? Was it the connection between home and school? Was it the connection among families of children in kindergarten? One parent later explained, "It started out with Janet wanting our input about what kinds of things we wanted the kids to learn throughout the year." Maybe that was all it took.

What I had originally intended to be a single meeting to identify learning priorities that might someday be embedded into the curriculum resulted in much more than I had expected. One meeting led to another and became a series of 10 ongoing work sessions to plan and prepare for real-life activities that would enrich, enhance, and extend the curriculum and influence the lives of many children and adults. At each meeting, we discussed more activities on the activity list. We had originally scheduled monthly meetings, but as we approached the end of the school year, families wanted to meet every two or three weeks to accomplish everything we had planned.

There was no formal agenda at the family meetings. Working through the activity lists provided a natural flow for our conversation. An item on the lists sparked the interest of someone and served as a catalyst for more discussion, helping us organize our thoughts and actions. One parent found that the activity lists "were great and served as a guide to help keep our discussion focused." Another thought the activity lists helped facilitate the discussion: "Janet would say, 'Okay, any ideas?' Someone would say something, and then we'd take that a little further. Everybody got involved."

The energy spread among the families, and the numbers began to grow. Here is how one parent described the enthusiasm: "That list, though, was the one thing because it got us interested, and if you can get people interested, they're going to come back to want to learn a little bit more. By the time that happens, perpetual motion just takes over. That's where we are now." Without realizing what had happened, we had become a team of adults working together to provide better educational opportunities for the children we shared. We were committed to perpetuating family involvement and supporting each other in our efforts.

As families became more engaged in their children's education, they began to assume new roles and responsibilities. Parent comments reflected a different way of thinking about teaching and learning and their changing roles in this process: "How can *we* incorporate that?" and "I'll do this and you can do that." Such comments reflected a truer collaboration and sense of shared responsibility.

Parents were beginning to see themselves as designers of curriculum, evident in this parent's comment: "I really like the fact that we get to have a say in what they do in kindergarten. . . . You work around whatever [Janet] has to teach. We just have input in how to do it, what kinds of things to do."

Parents recognized the effect their contributions were having on the teaching and learning in kindergarten. According to one parent, "Probably the most exciting part was all the ideas the parents came up with to meet the curriculum requirements. . . . and seeing how excited [Janet] was about everybody else's ideas. I think this is what really made it take off with all of us."

Family involvement really had taken off in kindergarten. Most families had become involved in their children's education in one way or another. Participating in evening meetings was just one avenue. Parents were spending time at home, at school, or in the community supporting their children's education. From the first meeting in November of only four parents to the last gathering in June, when more than 130 children and adults came together to celebrate their accomplishments, much had changed. These numbers reflect a significant connection between home and school. Perhaps it worked because we were all focused on the children, their learning, and the way the learning became part of their lives. But I still had questions:

• What effect did family involvement have on student learning?

• How did family involvement affect my

teaching?

• How did this involvement affect the families?

• Did the involvement have an effect on families' views about teaching and learning?

• How can I help the families who did not become involved?

As part of my research, I answered nearly all these questions through follow-up interviews with the families. Here I will share mostly what the parents did as codesigners and coteachers of the curriculum.

Parents as Codesigners of the Curriculum

Together, parents and I did more to improve children's learning than if we had worked separately, and the family meetings were a significant avenue for such improvement. Many parents identified the ABA Inventory as the catalyst that stimulated their thinking about teaching and learning and helped focus our work together during the meetings. For example, one parent said, "It all boils down to that very first sheet that she handed out. That kind of opened up our eyes, and that was the thing." Another parent explained, "I think that *the* way to get parents involved is that list, because it's broken down so well and it gives you so many different avenues of thinking. The list is a very good tool."

The children of 40 families were enrolled in my kindergarten classes. About 13 of those families were represented at most of the evening

meetings. An additional 13 families attended some of the meetings. The remaining 14 families were not at any of the meetings. Not attending the family meetings, however, does not imply that these families were not involved in their children's education.

The students' families represented varied cultural, socioeconomic, and educational backgrounds, as well as diverse family structures. Most children were living at home with both birth parents. In eight families, the parents were divorced or in the process of divorce. Of these eight families, five parents were remarried or living with a significant other. Grandparents were the legal guardians in three families. Single parents were raising their children in two families. Many of the children whose parents were attending meetings regularly were the first or only child in the family to enter the public school system. Other family members also participated, including aunts, uncles, and adult siblings. Specifically who attended and how often were not as important as the fact that family involvement reached well beyond the evening meetings, resulting in a more comprehensive model of family involvement than I had known in all my years of teaching.

Written communication among families was one of the most important strategies we discovered. After each meeting, a parent agreed to write a letter informing other families about our work together and inviting them to participate at home, at school, or in the community. At first, participants were reluctant to write the letters, but as time passed, they gladly accepted the responsibility. The sample letter shown in

Figure 3.1 captures the enthusiasm found in these letters.

Parents or grandparents wrote at least 15 letters. Each typically included a summary of the meeting; information about activities for learning at home, at school, and in the community; and an invitation for families to get involved in future meetings. Many of these letters communicated a willingness to do whatever possible to enable more families to attend.

Equally as important as the invitation was the appreciation and enthusiasm the writer expressed, such as, "Speaking of doing it all, we have planned and executed more than 40 activi-

---

3.1	Sample Parent/Guardian Letter

Greetings, Fellow Kindergarten Parents,

I want to recap the December meeting for the parents who were unable to attend. We had quite a turnout by combining both classes, and we decided to do this every month. Our next meeting is planned for January 8, so please mark that date and come join us at 6:00 p.m. (even if it means bringing the kids).

It's very rewarding for me to be involved with my son's education and the quality of that education. I'm sure most of you feel the same, but with work, the kids, the house, and everything that goes along with it, we kind of lose sight of things. That is why the meetings have been so rewarding for me. I get to know firsthand what my child will be doing and how it will be done.

As parents, we talk about what our kids do, how they act, and how they can learn to accomplish daily tasks—like getting them to sort laundry, wear their bike helmets, and learn values. Some of the events we have planned for this year are understanding bike safety, reinforcing the need to be wary of strangers, and learning to use 911 effectively. We have also decided to read a mystery book, have a holiday exchange of handmade gifts, and write to a kindergarten class in Germany. These ideas came from us—the parents—and what we would like to see our children learn, not only in school but also in the home.

So if you can spare an hour or so on January 8, come and join us. Your thoughts and suggestions are greatly valued by our little ones, and together we can make a difference in our children's lives. Hope to see you all at the meeting! If anyone needs a ride or has anything to share, but can't make it, please give me a call.

Sincerely,

[child's parent]

Used with permission.

ties this year. Go, team!" The family-to-family letters also shared personal thoughts about the future—for example, "As the end of the year quickly approaches, we are faced with the reality of getting split up and going to 1st grade. We have made many new friends, and we've learned quite a lot from each other in the year we've spent together. I'm sure next year will be no different from this year. Once we get in and get started, there will be no stopping us!"

It would have been impossible for me to write these letters. I could not have informed or invited family members with the same style or charm. As I reviewed the letters, I better understood the influence these parents had on one another and how passionate they were about our work together.

Parents as Coteachers

Those of us engaged in this collaboration believed our work was making a difference for the children. As one parent said, "It doesn't only have to do with school work. It has to do with the children's well-being." During the school year, we discussed more than 50 activities from the ABA lists in our family meetings. We planned and implemented more than 30 activities at school or in the community and recommended that many be carried out at home. Figure 3.2 shows a parent-generated list of activities that became the curriculum. We gave such lists to families of the kindergarten children. Parents created similar ones throughout the school year to inform families of our work together.

I also periodically summarized our work together. Figure 3.3, on page 50, shows a sample of learning activities families designed and taught. Notice how one activity from the list generated ideas for a number of additional activities. This figure illustrates how the ABA Inventory provided a frame for our work, but did not limit our creative thinking and planning.

Summarized in a table, the degree of involvement and amount of responsibility family members assumed are hard to see. The extent, of course, varied from family to family. Some adults participated in discussions and decision making even though they were not at the meetings. Some assumed responsibility for designing and delivering an entire learning activity, while others worked on only a part. One father's description of his classroom experience, shown in Figure 3.4, on page 53, suggests that no amount of involvement or investment in teaching and learning is too small.

Although the ways parents chose to become involved in delivering the curriculum—in teaching—varied, nearly all 40 families participated. At least 16 adults, representing 15 families, taught in our classroom regularly. Another 16 adults, representing 11 families, helped teach occasionally. Ten families focused on attending special events. Some of these families also accompanied the children on community outings. Most families attended parent-teacher conferences.

Only two families were not involved in at least one of these ways. We may never understand the barriers that made it more difficult for some than for others. Still, one of these two fami-

| 3.2 | Example of Parent-Generated Activities That Became the Curriculum |

These projects were discussed, researched, planned, or completely carried out by families.

Used the clock and calendar.

Completed daily schedule in class.

Posted cleanliness signs in bathrooms.

Made ID cards for children.

Presented a lesson on 911 (one grandfather was a retired fire chief).

Posted children-made signs around the school community to identify places in the school (e.g., for the restroom, office, library, and computer lab).

Designed an "office" center in the classroom with items families provided.

Arranged seating arrangements to build relationships between children.

Wrote to secret pals.

Structured a snack routine so that children could participate in food preparation and assume roles in setup, serving, and cleanup.

Encouraged children to share books from home through a book share program.

Purchased additional computer software for classroom and home use.

Arranged for additional computer time with adult support.

Arranged a bicycle safety class with Collins Cycle Shop.

Took a field trip to WISTEC Planetarium.

Purchased board games for classroom and home use.

Designed an extensive sewing project (made teddy bears).

Developed a project for students to collect junk and make hundreds of charts.

Purchased a Polaroid camera and used it.

Made plaster handprints of each child.

Shared nursery rhymes with children orally through read-alouds and videotapes.

Arranged for a presentation on bus safety.

Implemented use of homework notebooks.

Decorated grocery bags for Price Chopper grocery store.

Took a field trip to Price Chopper.

Collected food, clothing, toys, and books for donation to a homeless shelter.

Organized a presentation from First Place Families homeless shelter.

Took a field trip to a Pepsi bottling center.

lies demonstrated a strong commitment by making sure their child attended school regularly and by helping her with homework. As a consequence of this slightly less visible involvement, their daughter experienced substantial social, emotional, and academic growth. The other family attended our year-end celebration. While this effort was certainly the most limited involvement any of the 40 families exhibited, perhaps it promised a beginning that would grow in subsequent years.

Three Patterns of Family Involvement

Although family involvement varied, we identified three patterns in the ways family members supported their child's learning: teaching at school, in the community, and at home.

Teaching at School

When discussing their classroom involvement, many parents described their role as assisting the teacher and helping the children. They guided children through activities, presented new information or ideas, retaught skills and concepts I had introduced earlier, and worked with small groups or individual students. They always gave the children their time and attention. One mother explained, "I walk around from table to table. I listen to the teacher and follow her instructions. I try to be just another arm, another set of eyes and ears."

When I asked if she thought she did any of the teaching, she answered decisively, "No, I left that to the teacher." She elaborates, "I hear what she's telling them, [then] I'll spend a few minutes with a child and do what she says to help them through. But otherwise, I have no formal education in teaching." Although this mother did not label her work with the children as teaching, I would argue that the strategy she described is an effective method for teaching or reteaching concepts.

Classroom participation exceeded family members' expectations. Generally, they had not expected to become so involved in the children's learning, an idea reflected in this parent's comment: "It's more than I expected. I didn't expect to be there once a week, and I didn't expect a teacher to let me do as much as Janet has allowed us to do." Nor had they expected to become so interested in the lives and learning of children other than their own. As one parent observed, "I didn't realize that I would totally fall in love with *all* the kids. It's amazing to watch them learn."

Some families wanted to be more involved at school, but struggled to realize this commitment. As one parent related, "I expected to be more involved and I am not, but it is because of my work schedule. That was disappointing to me and still is. I struggle with that on a daily basis. I can't be as involved in school as I would like, because I have to provide for us in other ways."

Ironically, this same parent provided the children with one of their most memorable learning experiences. During a discussion at one of the family meetings, she offered to teach a lesson on germs. She carefully designed and presented a lesson, sharing basic information about germs, showing a brief video, and leading a discussion. She guided students in "de-germing" our classroom, using surgical gloves, masks, and spray bottles filled with disinfectant she had brought. High-quality involvement did not depend on quantity. This parent's contribution was substantial.

Repeatedly, parents provided learning experiences that would have been impossible for me to provide alone. Just having a number of adults in the classroom made a great difference to the children and their learning. Here is how one parent described the classroom environment: "I remember one time when I looked around, there were 20 children and probably 6 adults in the classroom. You had more parents in there and the ratio went down, so the kids had more one-on-one. I think that was a big help, too." The ratio may not always have been this high, but it was not uncommon for more than three adults to be in the classroom at any given time. Families had become an integral part of kindergarten teaching and learning.

Sometimes I was able to help a parent surmount barriers to classroom involvement. One mother rode the school bus to school, and I offered to take her home. The mother appreciated the extra effort and expressed a desire to become more involved: "We don't have a car or a phone. I'll probably end up more involved than I am now. Get my bike fixed and start coming over and see how [my daughter's] doing and

volunteering. It's fun for me. . . . It's like learning all over again." By my removing the transportation barrier, this parent became a more frequent classroom participant.

Teaching in the Community

Learning in the community is an effective strategy for helping children connect learning and life. For many families, this area of learning was a priority. Parents and grandparents wanted to create opportunities for children to learn outside the classroom and to bring the community into the classroom. They designed and delivered outings and presentations. Because these special events occurred only occasionally, they provided a convenient opportunity for working parents to become involved. Perhaps such lessons are also more interesting, because they help family members, as well as children, see more connections between learning and life.

One venture was an outing to a grocery store, an idea we first discussed at a family meeting. Parents and grandparents took the children to the store, where one of the fathers was the store manager. He and his coworkers guided us through the store. The tour was carefully planned to emphasize new experiences for the children, such as sampling uncommon fruits and vegetables, watching the butcher prepare several kinds of meat, and scanning and bagging their own snack foods. It was an extraordinary field trip that provided more than the obvious benefits. The store manager's wife showed her appreciation for the opportunity to show children

3.3	Activities Designed and Taught with Parents		

Activity from Age-Appropriate List	Ideas Generated	Parents' Roles and Responsibilities	Outcomes
Personal care: Responding to emergencies	Provide ID cards for children.	M— will inquire about organizations that make ID cards. Others will look for sample ID cards to bring to meeting.	M— designed a format for ID cards; wrote letter to families to gather data; and made the cards, including a photo and thumbprint for each child (with permission).
Personal business: Keeping or following a schedule	Discussed how children enjoy using calendars and schedules. Explore possibility of incorporating them into classroom routines.	Teacher will begin keeping a daily schedule with students.	Students assisted the teacher in writing and following a schedule of daily activities for the remainder of the school year.
Media: Books, newspapers, and magazines	Ask families to discuss favorite books and magazines with their child and to allow their child to share a publication with other students at the school—a book share.	H— will get book bags or folders for books. K— will draft a letter to parents explaining the book share program.	H— made book bags. Teacher sent a letter home to families explaining the book share. Students took turns bringing reading material from home.
Games, crafts, and hobbies: Sewing	Discussed children sewing stuffed animals.	H— will price supplies and bring a bear she made when she was in kindergarten to the next meeting. K— and H— will purchase supplies.	Students enjoyed sewing and stuffing bears with the guidance of many adults. The project fit nicely with a thematic study of animals.

3.3	Activities Designed and Taught with Parents—*continued*

Activity from Age-Appropriate List	Ideas Generated	Parents' Roles and Responsibilities	Outcomes
Games, crafts, and hobbies: Learning other languages and traditions	F— knows nursery rhymes in French; father-in-law knows Italian. Discussed the importance of exposing children to nursery rhymes.	Teacher will talk to other kindergarten teachers about incorporating nursery rhymes into curriculum plans. L— and M— will bring in audiotapes and videotapes with nursery rhymes.	Kindergarten classes studied nursery rhymes as part of a schoolwide thematic study of literary traditions. F— came to class and shared rhymes in French. A— prepared copies of rhymes in English and French for children to take home.
School membership and commitments: Doing homework	Discussed expanding the opportunities for home-school connections of student learning. One idea is to use homework to involve families more in their child's learning.	J— will purchase homework notebooks for students, and the teacher will write a letter to families explaining where the idea originated and details of homework procedures.	Homework notebooks became an important part of learning, with most children participating.
Community membership and commitments: Volunteering	Explained service learning projects, discussed ideas for possible projects, and reviewed student suggestions: The morning class would like to decorate grocery bags for shoppers. The afternoon class would like to give items to homeless people.	Students will make the final selection for service learning projects. R—, who manages a grocery store, offered to donate, display, and use decorated bags at the store. R— will also make arrangements for a field trip to the store if students choose this project. L— will research homeless shelters if students choose this project.	The morning students decorated grocery bags for shoppers. Students went on a field trip to deliver the grocery bags and to tour R—'s store. The afternoon students collected food, clothing, toys, and books to give to families in need. L— arranged for a representative from a homeless shelter to come talk to the class. Children loaded the collected items into a truck. The shelter representative offered to give students a tour of the shelter as a field trip, but the school declined.

what parents do in this comment: "My husband helped organize the field trip to his store. It's neat to have kids go to their parents' place of work just to get a general idea of what Mom and Dad are doing when they are away all day. It's one way to keep parents involved, and it is a learning experience at the same time."

Other remarkable community experiences followed. A grandmother planned and helped teach a lesson on bicycle safety given by a representative from a local cycle shop. A grandfather who was also a retired fire chief organized and taught a lesson about emergency procedures. As one parent said, "A teacher cannot do all that. They need some help, and I think our children's lives have been a lot better because of this." Indeed, families orchestrated and taught most of our community learning events. The field trips became more like family outings, with mothers, fathers, grandparents, and siblings joining in and sharing the experience.

Teaching at Home

Suggestions for how families could become involved in their children's learning at home came from my letters to the families and the letters that family members wrote to all student families. Such communications were a vital link between home and school. One parent remarked, "Keeping us informed about everything you're doing really helps. It involves parents whether they want to get involved or not. You send home the Monday envelope; it's got all the information in there. So they read it and they have to get involved."

Homework supported learning and connected home and school. I encouraged families to reinforce and expand on classroom learning experiences at home and in other places outside school. Families reported reviewing papers from school; reading books from the school library; participating in an at-home reading program; and working with letters, words, and number concepts. Some families went well beyond my suggestions. For example, one mom ordered a parenting magazine and read about how to do simple tasks with her daughter. She explained, "We look through the magazines . . . toys and food shopping ads and coupons, and she likes to look at the mail, too. So she can go through it and pick out the 'w' words and things for her homework."

Another parent related, "Education is everything. I've explained to my children that we are poor, so college is something you are going to have to earn and work for. . . . [Her daughter] loves school. She tells me about her whole day . . . all of it. . . . She enjoys it. She wanted to learn how to make her letters. Now her goal is to read. . . . I didn't really know how to begin teaching her, but Ms. Williams sends home all kinds of different homework . . . so it makes it much easier. . . . She looks at the pictures and kind of reads the little books [in the home reading program]. . . . I've been making lists of key words and having her write them. Words like *at* and *is*."

Parents, grandparents, siblings, and, in at least one instance, neighbors shared responsibility for supporting children at home. One child's mom described how she provided such an

| 3.4 | A Parent's Description of His Classroom Experience |

"I went in one day for about a half-hour to teach some nursery rhymes. We had been talking about different languages [at a family meeting]. . . . Ever since [our son] was a little baby, we used to put him to sleep by reciting some nursery rhymes in French. And his grandpa is Italian, so he would say some words in Italian. . . . Well, we were talking about that sheet [from the ABA Inventory] on languages. We had scribbled that sheet full the first time. We just wrote that [our son] knows nursery rhymes in French. Then when it [the meeting] came to [foreign] language, Janet said, 'Anything about that?'

" . . . So when it got to where they were doing a thing on nursery rhymes in class, I came into the classroom. . . . We all got in a circle and took off our shoes. We all sat there and did 'This Little Piggy Went to Market.' [My wife] had typed the English version on the computer, so they had all the words [for them] to share at home. Then I'd do the nursery rhyme in French. Then a couple of them would raise their hand, and they would just guess, and they would know it. It was just a kick seeing 22 kids and Ms. Williams sitting there on the floor. Then at the end of the day, when they went through what they liked about the day, a couple of them said they liked doing the nursery rhymes.

"Then I came in to pick up [our son] from school a couple of days later, and one of the little girls said, 'Can you do 'This Little Piggy' in that language again?' So I just sat there and I did it for her again. That's the thing that really shocked me: It's something that little—that goofy—and they liked it. When kids like the things they do at school, that's the way you want to get them started. Then down the road, if it's fun for them and if they enjoy it, as the years go by, they're going to like it even more. That's some satisfaction, just seeing a little child smile like that and get so much appreciation that took just a half-hour out of my day."

Used with permission.

opportunity: "We all live in the trailer park together, so they all play together. They're best friends, and sometimes they come down because they have the same homework and they do their homework together at the house. I'll just start gathering up supplies and we'll go sit on the couch at the coffee table. I've been a stay-at-home mom for 11 years, and it's fun to have something to do. I have a lot of time on my hands."

Next Steps Toward Ongoing Involvement

As the year ended, families started talking about how to stay involved. As a group, they hoped for similar relationships with future teachers and a continuation of shared responsibility in teaching and learning. Their wish is reflected in this parent's statement: "I would love for all teachers to be so caring and to ensure that parents are responsible for their children's education and are involved." Some parents began to strategize about how to keep the family meetings going in the future.

As families began to explore options for future involvement, they considered the parent-teacher organization (PTO) as an alternative. They recognized that the PTO had a schoolwide focus, but they were hopeful that their involvement would be meaningful and, as one parent said, would "take the place of some of what we have now." Another parent voiced caution about the PTO option, saying "The PTO—deep down inside, I really don't think that's what any of us really want, to be limited to that. The PTO is such a broad area, and you don't see immediate results. You're just not involved in what's happening in your kid's class."

Despite their enthusiasm, families recognized that their involvement might change as their children grew older. Rather than supporting children in the classroom, they would likely focus on schoolwide involvement. As one parent remarked, "I think your involvement will be more, not in the classroom as much, but maybe in the school more, a broader range. I think that when [the kids] get older, they want their own space and they don't want Mom or Dad hanging around. But you can help in the office or in the library or with school projects. I just think it'll shift a little bit." Thinking back to my colleagues' comments at the beginning of the year, I wondered if this shift was actually necessary, especially given other teachers' similar experiences when using the ABA Inventory to involve families with classrooms in higher grades.

I shared the parents' hopes for the future, and I also planned to continue building similar relationships with new families. I, too, wanted a repeat of our year together. One parent offered this bit of advice: "Let the new group of parents grow at their own pace—not show them what it should be or what it will be, but let them grow at their own pace." So as the next year started, we began new meetings with a new group of children and their families. We worked toward the same goal: providing a high-quality education for the children in kindergarten. The cycle continues.

Final Reflections

I concluded that my effort to better involve families worked. By the end of the year, even the most reluctant families participated—some more actively or visibly than others. But the most important lesson this project taught me was that all families can become involved in their children's education, and such involvement makes a difference in the lives of the children.

It also made differences for the adults. I certainly changed. The richness of ideas and opportunities our work afforded the children would have been impossible for me to provide single-handedly. When I began thinking about this change in my practice, I worried that I wouldn't be able to develop meaningful relationships with all the families. But as one of the parents observed, "I think there are parents who are afraid and there are teachers who are afraid.

And that's what's hard—getting them together." I'm glad I overcame my fears.

The parents changed as well. They developed new relationships with their children, other parents' children, each other, and me. One father described the relationships he developed with children in his son's class and the fondness with which he watched them grow: "That's a neat thing—you see them out in public and they wave and smile. . . . It's amazing to see how much all of them have grown, how much all of them have changed. That's what's neat." Another mother said, "We became a support group, not just with what was going on in school, but what we were dealing with in our kids—how the changes in their lives were affecting them. It was nice to know that everybody else was going through stuff like that."

In the end, the families and I learned that with family involvement, the whole was greater than the sum of the parts, and much greater than any one part alone. Working together toward a common goal brought great strength and richness to our effort. Our efforts were sustained over time as parents became increasingly involved in the school. Such involvement is reflected in the principal's comments in Figure 3.5.

3.5	A Principal's Comments

The students who were in Janet's class during the year described in this chapter are now in 3rd grade. The parents who became most regularly and actively involved in the kindergarten family meetings remain the most active parents in school governance as site council representatives and fund-raising volunteers.

Monthly parent-teacher organization (PTO) meetings typically attract 30–35 parents. About half of those who attend come regularly, and virtually all of those in active leadership roles are parents whose children started their formal schooling in Janet's kindergarten class.

Nancy McCullum, Principal
Danebo Elementary School

Used with permission.

For Further Reading

Williams found the following references helpful in her work as a researcher and teacher.

Aronson, J. Z. (1996). How schools can recruit hard-to-reach parents. *Educational Leadership, 53*(7), 58–60.

Boyer, E. (1995). *The basic school: A community for learning.* Princeton, NJ: The Carnegie Foundation for the Advancement of Teaching.

Comer, J. P., Haynes, N. M., Joyner, E. T., & Ben-Avie, M. (Eds.). (1996). *Rallying the whole village: The Comer process for reforming education.* New York: Teachers College Press.

Daniels, H. (1996). The best practice project: Building parent partnerships in Chicago. *Educational Leadership, 53*(7), 38–43.

Dodd, A. W. (1996). Involving parents, avoiding gridlock. *Educational Leadership, 53*(7), 44–46.

Ferguson, P. M., & Squires, J. (1998). Strengthening the linkages between schools and families of children with disabilities. *Oregon School Studies Council Bulletin.* Eugene: College of Education, University of Oregon.

Floyd, L. (1998). Joining hands: A parental involvement program. *Urban Education, 33*(1), 123–135.

Okagaki, L., & Frensch, P. A. (1998). Parenting and children's school achievement: A multiethnic perspective. *American Educational Research Journal, 35*(1), 123–144.

Sanders, M. G., & Epstein, J. L. (1998). *School-family-community partnerships in middle and high schools: From theory to practice. Report No. 22.* Baltimore: Center for Research on the Education of Students Placed at Risk.

Recommended Web Site

http://PFIE.ed.gov/The Partnership for Family Involvement in Education increases opportunities for families to be more involved in their children's learning at school and at home, and to use family-school-community partnerships to strengthen schools and improve student achievement.

Planning for Everyone and Each One

The direction and commitment of the current multiple reform efforts are to reinvent schools as places of learning that respond to individual student differences and interests within the context of the classroom and school community. For many teachers, such work isn't as difficult as it sounds. Good teachers are good, at least in part, because of their ability to address a single child's uniqueness while managing the ebb and flow of the whole class. Good teachers have always been able to move rapidly between the big picture of the whole class and the single child.

Most of us remember the few teachers in our own learning history who fielded the question we really wanted to ask, let us change the assignment so we could do something we thought was really special, and generally inspired us to produce our best efforts. Some of us also remember that these teachers accomplished this powerful singling out in a way that made us feel "proud special" instead of "sorry special."

As special education gradually funneled more students away from the general education classroom, some general education teachers became less practiced at accommodating certain student differences, yet remained able to tailor their teaching and planning for others. "Human diversity" acquired narrower definitional limits, at least within the learning community of the general education classroom. "Sorry special" became the more dominant description of how children felt in response to efforts to help them learn better or differently in places outside the general education classroom.

For most general education teachers, reinventing teaching and learning means discovering anew how to stretch their planning creativity to accommodate more different kinds of "each ones." For special educators, the stretching is different. They need to think first about the whole general education class and how learning activities in it can provide rich opportunities for students they used to teach alone—rather than thinking about the individual child and how that child might, or might not, fit in to the activities of a larger group.

In this chapter, we offer four planning tools to help both general and special educators stretch: a long-range planning web, a long-range curriculum plan, a long-range teaching plan, and a daily or weekly teaching plan. We begin by explaining why collaborative curriculum planning may be difficult for general and special educators.

Competing Approaches to Planning

We realize that, for teachers, *planning* is really just an effort to gain some amount of comfort with the chaos. Plans, especially for general educators, impose some order and direction, but are rarely expected to unfold as anticipated. Teaching plans are meant to be changed; they provide enough structure so that changes will be for the better more often than for the worse. Special educators sometimes forget this essential unpredictability and become constrained rather

than aided by their plans. This is one difference that can make it challenging for general and special education teachers to begin working together, but there are others.

Within special education, educators have relied, at least since the mid-1970s, upon creating detailed annual plans for each student's curriculum and teaching. Although these individualized education plans (IEPs) meet many accountability requirements of both federal and state regulations, they often do not serve teachers well. Special educators find themselves spending hours stretching into days creating IEPs, which are then filed away until the annual process gears up again 9 to 10 months later. General educators approach the IEP document with consternation and suspicion, seen in such comments as, "Do I really have to do this?" "How do I do this and teach the rest of the class?" "I don't know what I'm going to teach in March exactly, and I can't really say what this student might be able to learn as part of that unit."

General educators generally plan for longer periods of time in broader strokes, leaving the detailed lesson planning to right before, and even during, their teaching. They also tend to start their planning from the broader view of the whole class rather than from any one child's learning perspective. *Special educators plan from the student to the class, while general educators plan from the class to the student.* In classrooms with much diversity, one or the other approach doesn't work as well as both together.

How Can General Educators and Special Educators Plan Together?

If students with disabilities, who must have detailed and annual IEPs, are to become fully included as learning members of a general education classroom, changes in the process for generating IEPs need to occur. We suggest an approach that takes advantage of the planning strengths of both types of educators. Such a process generates curriculum goals annually (as now required by IEP regulations), but leaves the articulation of specific teaching objectives until teachers are closer to the teaching event. This seemingly small change has advantages:

• Teaching objectives can be more responsive to student learning. One problem teachers find with writing annual objectives is that an IEP is not always responsive to changes in a student's learning. An IEP is only a teacher's best guess about what and how much the student might learn. When a best guess is even a little off the mark, the IEP becomes less useful as a guide to teaching. The most effective, flexible, and efficient teachers constantly revise teaching objectives in response to students' work and learning. Thus teaching objectives written close to the teaching event are most likely to reflect *exactly* what is transpiring with the student's learning.

• Teaching objectives can better reflect the curriculum. Because general education teachers usually make their curricular decisions only the week, day, or even hours before actually teach-

ing, annual teaching objectives must be written in general terms. Teachers find it difficult to apply these generally worded objectives to the specific teaching situations they are designing. Students may be left out, or teachers may ask another adult to figure out what a particular student should be doing. If teaching objectives are written close to the teaching event, student learning can be framed in terms of the content, clearly showing everyone how students will participate and what they will be expected to accomplish.

• The IEP becomes a working document. The first two advantages result in the IEP becoming something teachers use all the time to help them make and record their curricular decisions. The IEP-in-a-drawer becomes the IEP-in-the-hand, constantly reminding all teachers involved with the class what they are trying to accomplish for those students whose successful learning requires more careful tailoring and personalizing.

A Long-Range Curriculum Plan

This tool can be used by groups of teachers working on long-term planning to achieve curricular aims over weeks or months. Instead of just "following the book," teachers are getting together to engage in this kind of creative and collaborative curricular planning. First, they identify broad curricular themes that might be either conceptual (e.g., conflict, culture, and growth) or substantive (e.g., relationships and animals). These themes provide coherence and constancy as students move from one learning activity to the next. Themes also invigorate skill-based learning, such as reading, math, and writing, by making such learning more interesting and meaningful.

Such a tool draws on webbing to expand the theme into a wide variety of possible topics that can be clustered into learning activities. Webbing is a brainstorming technique familiar to most general educators, but it may not be as familiar to special educators. Some general education teachers use webbing with their students to involve them in curriculum design and learning activities.

Wednesday afternoons are designated for team planning at Grandview. Ms. Clark and her colleagues meet in her classroom, sitting around the oval table, usually with cookies and coffee. Brainstorming generates ideas for the next unit from the "Ancient Civilizations" part of the curriculum and soon settles on Egypt as the focus of the unit. Mr. West, the librarian at Grandview, begins by listing available literature, Web sites, and videos. Ms. Clark mentions two book titles that she's seen repeatedly in examples of thematic plans on this topic. She asks for feedback on the books' reading levels. Ms. Simpson, the reading specialist, and Ms. Dean, the educational assistant, offer to help figure out the reading levels and explore additional options at different levels. Ms. Jackson, the speech-language specialist, suggests vocabulary mapping to match the textbook and generate a fuller list of possible words for the class.

The group continues to add ideas until the cookies are gone and the planning web is nearly full. Figure 4.1 shows the completed long-range

planning web that the team devised; it reflects all benchmark areas that need to be addressed in the 6th grade. Notice that the broad theme of "Egypt" naturally generated a variety of topics and activities that might take from an hour to several days or even a couple of weeks to cover.

Another Wednesday afternoon found the same group back at Ms. Clark's oval table to use the long-range planning web to develop a long-range curriculum plan. They began to identify specific academic benchmark targets and consider implications for individual students. Such work will enable them to link teaching activities directly to learning standards for all students. This big picture, broad-stroke planning also helps team members identify and share responsibility for organizing their work. Figure 4.2 shows how the work was divided up.

Notice that the group has identified additional tasks for needed resources, such as creating study guides, reserving the computer lab for extra time, and collecting magazines and travel brochures. Long-range planning has helped the group think about supports Ms. Clark's 29 students will need for this particular unit. Team members have begun to identify several clusters of students who will need additional thought or special attention. They have even started to pair up students into teams. It is not always clear to an outsider exactly why these teachers have singled out or paired these students, but it does seem clear that the teachers intend to spend more time organizing their thinking about how activities will need to be tailored to be successful for those students.

4.1 Example of a Long-Range Planning Web

Date: *December 1999*

Team Members: *Ms. Clark, Ms. Jackson, Ms. Simpson, Ms. Dean, Mr. West*

Time Frame for Plan: *8 weeks*

Months: *February/March*

Year: *2000*

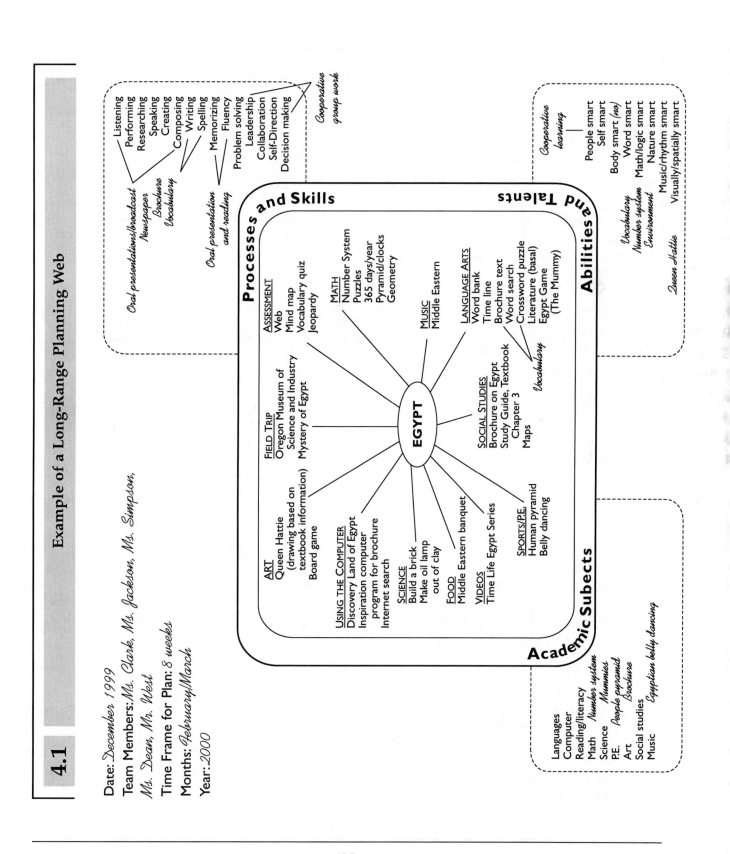

Processes and Skills

Listening
Performing
Researching
Speaking
Creating
Composing
Writing
Spelling
Memorizing
Fluency
Problem solving
Leadership
Collaboration
Self-Direction
Decision making

Cooperative group work

Oral presentation/broadcast
Newspaper
Brochure
Vocabulary

Oral presentation and reading

Abilities and Talents

Cooperative learning

People smart
Self smart
Body smart *(no)*
Word smart
Math/logic smart
Nature smart
Music/rhythm smart
Visually/spatially smart

Vocabulary
Number system
Environment

Queen Hattie

Academic Subjects (center web)

EGYPT

ASSESSMENT
Web
Mind map
Vocabulary quiz
Jeopardy

MATH
Number System
Puzzles
365 days/year
Pyramid/clocks
Geometry

MUSIC
Middle Eastern

LANGUAGE ARTS
Word bank
Time line
Brochure text
Word search
Crossword puzzle
Literature (basal)
Egypt Game
(The Mummy)

Vocabulary

SOCIAL STUDIES
Brochure on Egypt
Study Guide, Textbook
Chapter 3
Maps

SPORTS/P.E.
Human pyramid
Belly dancing

VIDEOS
Time Life Egypt Series

FOOD
Middle Eastern banquet

SCIENCE
Build a brick
Make oil lamp
out of clay

USING THE COMPUTER
Discovery Land of Egypt
Inspiration computer
program for brochure
Internet search

FIELD TRIP
Oregon Museum of
Science and Industry
Mystery of Egypt

ART
Queen Hattie
(drawing based on
textbook information)
Board game

Academic Subjects

Languages
Computer
Reading/literacy
Math *Number system*
Science *Mummies*
P.E. *People pyramid*
Art *Brochure*
Social studies
Music *Egyptian belly dancing*

4.2 — Example of a Long-Range Curriculum Plan

Date: *January 2000*   Grade Level: *6*

Team Members: *Ms. Clark, Ms. Jackson, Ms. Simpson, Ms. Dean, Mr. West*

Class Snapshot (e.g., student interests and preferences, cultural affiliations, learning styles, and abilities):
- *Two social studies classes; 60 students total.* • *At least two English as a second language students.*
- *Several students have IEPs; need to buddy-up.* • *Most students like to do hands-on activities.*
- *At least two students have trouble staying on task; need to buddy-up.* • *Some students work well—are fast learners; they need some extra activities.*

Curriculum Themes:

Type of Activity	Lead Person	Resource Implications	Implications for Individual Students
Integrated curriculum *Vocabulary webbing*	*Ms. Jackson*	*Use Inspiration software program for web/overhead.*	*Picture webs for Jamie, Susannah, and Brandon.*
Guided reading	*Ms. Clark*	*Create study guides.*	*Buddy work* *Josh/Bill*
Watch video; do research on the Internet	*Mr. West* *Ms. Simpson*	*Reserve computer lab, reserve video, and put hold on books.*	*Eli/Maria* *Tasha/Susannah* *Josiah/Ben*
Brochures	*Ms. Jackson* *Ms. Clark* *Ms. Dean*	*Collect magazines and travel brochures.*	*Katie/Mary* *Brandon/Miguel* *Jamie/Becky*
Academic focus *Social studies—benchmarks* *Learning chronological order* *Comparing cultural characteristics* *Recognizing geographic locations* *Language arts* *Reading strategies* *Locating information* *Analyzing or evaluating information* *Extending or comprehending information* *Communication* *Conveying main ideas* *Sequencing information clearly* *Developing oral fluency*			

Moving to a Long-Range *Teaching* Plan

Long-range planning for teaching is intertwined with long-range planning for curriculum. Curriculum decisions *are* teaching decisions, and ongoing teaching decisions constitute the real curriculum in use. A long-range teaching plan encourages groups of teachers to think broadly and expansively about all the options they have for making the learning experience as exciting and responsive as possible to all their students. For any one integrated curriculum activity or academic focus activity thought up during broad stroke curriculum planning, teachers have many teaching choices.

A long-range teaching plan prompts teachers to first make their curriculum/teaching decisions within a set of teaching dimensions, and then to think about the implications of their decisions as they develop their own task list and student learning activities. Figure 4.3 shows an example of such a plan. The plan's format encourages teachers to think not only about their expectations for student learning, but also about other aspects of teaching planning, such as, Where would be the best locations for this lesson? Are there ways I can enhance the environmental conditions? For example, during one of the videos for the Egypt unit, Ms. Clark could turn up the thermostat to simulate desert heat.

The long-range teaching plan can be reformatted and copied onto a set of cards. Figure 4.4 is a sample planning card, showing the types of information that teachers should consider as they think through the curriculum design process.

Teachers can use the cards to pl[...] the curriculum units sketched o[...] long-range curriculum planning[...] This plan encourages "thinking[...] than "filling out," though many[...] plan to make notes that will late[...] recapture their decisions.

Like the long-range curricul[...] teaching plan can help teachers [...] those students who will require [...] and focused decisions if their le[...] ences are to be tailored well eno[...] achieve the kind of active, mean[...] tion in community life that educ[...] value.

After developing the long-ra[...] plan, Ms. Clark's planning grou[...] focus to consider the long-range [...] The format allowed the group to[...] planning cycle and better relate [...] tations for the Egypt unit to real-[...] where students could apply this [...] Clark has found that she can oft[...] range teaching plan and move st[...] web to more detailed lesson plar[...] ing on the team members and th[...] this instance, using the long-rang[...] shown in Figure 4.3 helped Ms. [...] communicate academic expectati[...] Egypt unit to the special educatic[...] who were still working on stude[...] working through this step, teach[...] that IEPs will include goals refle[...] content of the Egypt unit.

This planning session worke[...] details of activity and teaching o[...]

ers will likely do more of this kind of
led brainstorming, planning, readjusting,
eplanning as they proceed with the unit.
rtheless, they have developed a teaching
that includes general strategies for all stu-
s, including those with diverse needs.

w Does Long-Range nning Work for IEP dents?

well long-range planning works depends
ow services for students officially designated
ligible for special education" are organized.
y schools are in a time of transition. Only
e schools and districts have completely
rbed previously separate special education

in ways that preserve all the functions, but without any of the labels. Such labels can be disability
labels or other kinds of labels signaling different
educational needs that grow out of cultural and
linguistic differences.

When schools are unified and inclusive practices are common and comprehensive, all students are assigned to general education classrooms supported by groups of teachers. Each
teacher has different teaching strengths and
preparation. At least one has a history of interest
and preparation in tailoring curriculum for more
challenging learners and providing the additional supports they might require. In such reinvented, inclusive situations, the two types of plans
(Figures 4.2 and 4.3) help identify students that
might need more systematic discussion, detailed
planning, and support.

.3	Example of a Long-Range Teaching Plan

Curriculum Area/Aim/Theme/Unit/Lesson: *Ancient Egypt*

pe of Activity*	Related Real-Life Activities
ring for self, ends, and family	*Carry out a home responsibility (e.g., clean with old and new techniques).* *Cook a meal (e.g., plan and prepare a Middle Eastern banquet).*
ontributing to mmunity	*Construct and problem-solve (e.g., work in groups to problem-solve constructing a pyramid).*
joying leisure d recreation	*Take a trip (e.g., view King Tut exhibit in person or on the Web).* *Do an arts and crafts activity (e.g., make a mosaic trivet or weave a basket).* *Read for pleasure (e.g., go to the library to find an Egyptian mystery to read).*

three types of activities are from the ABA Age-Appropriate Activity Lists described in Chapter 2.

| 4.3 | Example of a Long-Range Teaching Plan—*continued* |

Plan Summary		Special Considerations*
Expectations for students: Understand importance and contributions of ancient Egyptian culture Make a map of the area Develop and comprehend new vocabulary	**Lesson materials:** Textbooks Videos Library books Art materials Software (Inspiration)	**Goals:** Key vocabulary translated for Maria and Miguel. Easily manipulated craft supplies for Tasha. Becky and Samuel to buddy-read with low readers. Working on time management. Cooperating, interacting, and working with others.
Lesson design and format: Minilectures Buddy learning Guest presentation Computer-assisted instruction	**Environmental conditions:** Use another classroom for space to spread out Use outside space (brick building) Use music to mask noise	
Locations: Classroom Computer lab Art room Library School kitchen Gym Oregon Museum of Science and Industry	**Extra/Outside resources:** Go on field trip to Oregon Museum of Science and Industry. Invite people from community to speak (e.g., belly dancer or architect)	
Activity and lesson plan flow: Introduce vocabulary on cards Show a video Read a literature book Assign projects Play puzzles and games Assess progress		

*Examples: Students who use IEPs, who are talented and gifted, who use English as a second language, and who leave early for other classes or activities.

4.4 Sample Planning Card

What environmental considerations need to be considered?

Time of day

Length of lesson activity

Room temperature and lighting

Environmental noises and other distractions

Sequence with other daily lessons, activities, and events

What applies in this case?
What are implications for groups of students and for individual students?

How will this lesson accommodate student learning differences?

Cognitively:
Memory
Problem solving
Organization
Speed
Logical-mathematical
Linguistic
Musical/aesthetic
Spatial relations
Bodily-kinesthetic
Inter- and intrapersonal

Affectively:
Persistence
Peer collaboration
Dealing with errors
Responsibility
Leadership
Activity
Thinking
Emotion

What applies in this case?
What are implications for groups
of students and for individual students?

In Sum:

Have I considered:
Lesson materials
Lesson design and format
Locations
Activity or lesson plan
Student expectations
Environmental conditions

Do I need to personalize the
work for individuals or groups?

Teachers may find themselves in somewhat less inclusive situations during this period of school change. "Special" students are still served by a separate system. Some might be assigned only part-time to general education classrooms and spend the rest of their time in other places, such as resource rooms or self-contained classrooms. Others might be assigned full-time to general education classrooms, but bring the special-only aspects of a separate curriculum and teaching approach along with them to the classroom in the form of another adult who takes primary responsibility for their learning. These are examples of *integration*. Although integration is a step on the way to truly reinvented, inclusive schools, it still maintains much of the separateness that can lead to more feelings of "sorry special" than of "proud special" in students.

For situations characterized as integration, the long-range curriculum plan can help special education teachers and assistants learn what might be happening in general education settings they are trying to make more inclusive. General education teachers would complete the plan and give it to the specialist team before any kind of IEP meeting is held. The information sketched on the plan might help the IEP participants construct annual goals that better reflect the general education curriculum.

If the general education teacher doesn't complete a plan, special educators might use the long-range teaching plan as an interview guide to gather information about the classrooms they are integrating their students into. They would not only collect information that might help them more successfully integrate their students,

but also send a message to the general education teacher that they are trying to learn about that teacher's decisions. Too often, general education teachers on the receiving end of integration get the message that special educators want to change them to look more "special" so the labeled student will fit in. By beginning with the general education teacher's planning decisions, the special educator encourages a more collaborative working relationship. Over time, general education teachers may adopt the long-range teaching plan format and begin using it more routinely as a thinking guide.

A Daily or Weekly Lesson Plan

The same day Ms. Clark and her team thought through the long-range teaching plan, they also began to zero in on a specific lesson and finalize the details of a teaching design. The lesson plan shown in Figure 4.5 provided a template for Ms. Clark to sequence her teaching, identify materials, and establish a time frame. This tool encourages the most detailed planning, including envisioning how the lesson will flow from the teacher's first effort to hook the class into the topic, through the work of the lesson, to the close and transition to the next lesson or activity.

Notice in the figure that individual student expectations are noted to the side of the lesson plan. The plan could easily be shared between classroom teacher and support staff for additional reminders and suggestions. As Ms. Clark's team thought about individual student needs,

4.5   Example of a Lesson Plan

Date: *March 2000*
Theme: *Ancient Egypt*
Unit or Lesson: *Social Studies and Language Arts*

Process or Skills:
Improve auditory and written comprehension.
Understand importance of accuracy.
Engage in cooperative learning.

What We Will Do	Special Considerations*
Activity: Queen Hattie Project *Use social studies text to compile a list of coronation regalia and create a drawing of Hattie, including as many details as possible.*	*Buddy-up Samuel and Tasha. Create a small group with a peer assistant reading to Josh, Brandon, Maria, Jamie, and Susannah.*
Introduction (hook and stated purpose): *Show video. Instruct students how to watch for details (e.g., dress and art). Ask them to brainstorm a pharaoh (what he looks like and what he wears). Then ask them to consider the pharaoh as a woman.*	

Development (activity, guided practice, modeling, student practice, and reteaching):
  Students read text individually or in pairs.
  Each student compiles a list of ceremonial garb.
  Each student draws a rendition of Queen Hattie in her finery.
  Students may add other details, such as Egyptian artwork and pyramids, for extra credit.
	Allow Brandon to help kids who need it.
	
	Provide a traceable picture if needed.

Closure (tie lesson together, review homework, draw a picture, and make a journal entry):
  Students score each other's work by counting details.
  Display drawings.
	Provide a list on an overhead projector to show details to look for; give oral instructions.

Time and material:
  Three social studies periods.
  Drawing paper, colored pencils, extra books, hieroglyphics pages, and rulers.	

*Examples: Students who use IEPs, who are talented and gifted, who use English as a second language, and who leave early for other classes or activities.

Ms. Clark realized that some students might be creatively and artistically challenged by the Queen Hattie project. They might get stuck on the artwork and give up, or be too discouraged to try to be creative. She decided to offer a traceable picture from an old worksheet to help such students get unstuck.

As the lesson turned out, two boys needed the traceable picture and willingly continued the activity with this support. Becky asked Brandon for help with ideas to get her started, and his pride at being able to assist filled the room as he sat down to help.

* * *

In this chapter, we described long-range planning for curriculum and both long-range and short-term planning for teaching. We offered two heuristic tools to help with curriculum planning (a long-range curriculum plan and a long-range planning web) and three tools to help with lesson planning (a long-range teaching plan, a daily or weekly lesson plan, and a sample planning card). Long-range planning gets the process started with divergent brainstorming, while the long-range curriculum plan adds detail by sketching the big curricular picture with broad strokes for everyone in the class. Sample planning cards help teachers think through the curriculum design process. The long-range teaching plan helps fill in the details closer to the teaching event to highlight the curricular and teaching decisions for students who might require focused attention. Some students may require additional decisions to further enrich, enhance, overlap, and

embed teaching objectives and activities. The lesson plan prompts even more of these individual student decisions. Trying to anticipate what might go wrong, as Ms. Clark did when she thought about who might get stuck, is as important an aspect of lesson planning as figuring out the hook, flow, and outcomes.

For Further Reading

In today's classrooms and schools, diversity is the norm. Students from many different personal, cultural, and economic situations—and with a variety of learning characteristics and needs—are being educated together. The following resources may help teachers when thinking and planning to meet the needs of this diverse population: Cole (1995); Kameenui and Carnine (1998); Ford (1997); Ford, Obiakor, and Patton (1995); Freedman, Simons, Kalnin, Careno, and the M-Class Teams (1999); Gersten and Baker (2000); and Koss-Chiono and Vargas (1999).

As classrooms become more diverse, curriculum and instruction will also need to be more varied and inclusive in content and strategy. These works provide a number of ideas for teaching in today's diverse classrooms: Daniels (1994); Jarrett (1999); Johnson (1995); Margulies (1991, 1993); Noe and Johnson (1999); Schifter (1996); and Schifter and Fosnot (1993).

Teachers and other school personnel are also realizing that they can no longer work alone to accomplish their goals for students. But sometimes, it's difficult to figure out how to work together, much less to find the time. The following works may be helpful when teachers are thinking about how to find the time to collaborate: Ferguson (1999); Ginsberg, Johnson, and Moffett (1997); Maeroff (1993); and Stanovich (1996).

Cole, R. W. (Ed.). (1995). *Educating everybody's children: Diverse teaching strategies for diverse learners.* Alexandria, VA: Association for Supervision and Curriculum Development.

Daniels, H. (1994). *Literature circles: Voice and choice in the student-centered classroom.* York, ME: Stenhouse Publishers.

Ferguson, D. L. (1999). *On working together: Groupwork, teamwork, and collaborative work among educators.* Denver, CO: National Institute for Urban School Improvement.

Ford, B. A. (1997). *Multiple voices for ethnically diverse exceptional learners.* Reston, VA: Council for Exceptional Children.

Ford, B. A., Obiakor, F. E., & Patton, J. M. (Eds.). (1995). *Effective education of African American exceptional learners.* Austin, TX: Pro-Ed., Inc.

Freedman, S. W., Simons, E. R., Kalnin, J. S., Careno, A., & the M-Class Teams. (1999). *Inside city schools: Investigating literacy in multicultural classrooms.* New York: Teachers College Press.

Gersten, R., & Baker, S. (2000). *An overview of instructional practices for English-language learners: Prominent themes and future directions.* Denver, CO: National Institute for Urban School Improvement.

Ginsberg, M. B., Johnson, J. F., Jr., & Moffett, C. A. (1997). *Educators supporting educators: A guide to organizing school support teams.* Alexandria, VA: Association for Supervision and Curriculum Development.

Jarrett, D. (1999). *The inclusive classroom: Mathematics and science instruction for students with learning disabilities. It's just good teaching.* Portland, OR: Northwest Regional Educational Laboratory.

Johnson, K. (1995). Exploring the world with private eye. *Educational Leadership, 53*(1), 52–55.

Kameenui, E. J., & Carnine, D. W. (1998). *Effective teaching strategies that accommodate diverse learners.* Des Moines, IA: Prentice-Hall.

Koss-Chiono, J. D., & Vargas, L. A. (1999). *Working with Latino youth: Culture, development, and context.* San Francisco: Jossey-Bass.

Maeroff, G. I. (1993). *Team building for school change: Equipping teachers for new roles.* New York: Teachers College Press.

Margulies, N. (1991). *Mapping inner space: Learning and teaching mind mapping.* Tucson, AZ: Zephyr Press.

Margulies, N.(1993). *Maps, mindscapes, and more* [videotape]. Tucson, AZ: Zephyr Press.

Noe, K. L. S., & Johnson, N. J. (1999*). Getting started with literature circles. The Bill Harp Professional Teachers Library Series.* Norwood, MA: Christopher-Gordon Publishers.

Schifter, D. (Ed.). (1996). *What's happening in math class? Volume 1: Envisioning new practices through teacher narratives. Series on school reform.* New York: Teachers College Press.

Schifter, D., & Fosnot, C. T. (1993). *Reconstructing mathematics education: Stories of teachers meeting the challenge of reform.* New York: Teachers College Press.

Stanovich, P. J. (1996). Collaboration—The key to successful instruction in today's inclusive schools. *Intervention in School and Clinic, 32*(1), 39–42.

Recommended Web Sites

http://www.asha.org/The American Speech-Language-Hearing Association (ASHA) is the professional and scientific association for speech-language pathologists; audiologists; and speech, language, and hearing scientists in the United States and internationally. Its mission is to promote the interests of and provide the highest quality services for professionals in audiology, speech-language pathology, and speech and hearing science, and to advocate for people with communication disabilities.

http://www.arts.gov/The National Endowment for the Arts nurtures the expression of human creativity, supports cultivation of community spirit, and fosters recognition and appreciation of the excellence and diversity of artistic accomplishments in the United States.

http://www.synapseadaptive.com/inspiration/beta.html Inspiration® is a software program to help students structure their research or work. Students can create concept maps, webs, and other graphical organizers; set priorities; and rearrange ideas. For more ideas on how to integrate Inspiration into your classroom, see the book *Classroom Ideas Using Inspiration: For Teachers by Teachers* at http://www.synapseadaptive.com/inspiration/thebook.html.

http://www.nsf.gov/start.htm The National Science Foundation is an independent U.S. government agency responsible for promoting science and engineering through programs that invest more than $3.3 billion per year in almost 20,000 research and education projects in science and engineering.

http://www.nea.org/The National Education Association (NEA) is the oldest and largest organization in the United States committed to advancing the cause of public education. NEA members work at every level of education, from preschool to university graduate programs. NEA has affiliates in every state as well as in over 13,000 local communities across the United States.

http://www.naeyc.org/The National Association for the Education of Young Children (NAEYC) is an organization of early childhood professionals dedicated to improving the quality of early childhood education programs for children birth through age 8. NAEYC's primary goals are to improve professional practice and working conditions in early childhood education and build public understanding and support for high-quality early childhood programs.

http://www.nctm.org/mt/2000/04/*Mathematics Teacher Online* is an official journal of the National Council of Teachers of Mathematics. It is devoted to improving mathematics education from grade 8 through two-year and teacher education colleges.

http://www.ed.gov/americacounts/America Counts is guided by six strategic goals: equip teachers to teach challenging mathematics through high-quality preparation and ongoing professional growth; provide personal attention and additional learning time for students; support high-quality research to inform about best practices of mathematics teaching and learning; build public understanding of the mathematics today's students must master; encourage a challenging and engaging curriculum for all students, based on rigorous standards; and promote the coordinated and effective use of federal, state, and local resources.

http://www.ncbe.gwu.edu/about.htm The National Clearinghouse for Bilingual Education (NCBE) is funded by the U.S. Department of Education's Office of Bilingual Education and Minority Languages Affairs to collect, analyze, and disseminate information on the effective education of linguistically and culturally diverse learners in the United States.

http://www.the-private-eye.com/ruef/html/home.htm The Private Eye is a program that highlights the drama and wonder of looking closely at the world, thinking by analogy, changing scale, and theorizing. Designed to develop higher-order thinking skills, creativity, and scientific literacy across subjects, it's based on a simple set of "tools" that produce "gifted results."

http://www.readnaturally.com/The Read Naturally program provides a method to improve reading fluency. Most struggling readers have fluency problems and spend little time reading. The program combines three powerful strategies for improving fluency: teacher modeling, repeated reading, and progress monitoring.

Achieving Balance with Mixed-Ability Learning Groups

Teachers traditionally have organized their students by applying an assumption of homogeneity: Students who share the same or similar learning characteristics or abilities learn best when grouped together. Most teachers also learned to organize their teaching according to this kind of ability grouping. Such a strategy permits teachers to tailor instruction to student ability while avoiding the demands of fully individualized, or even individually adapted, teaching.

Homogeneous grouping may still be a good choice on some learning occasions and for some learning tasks. But an increasing number of teachers are finding that their students are too different for this type of strategy to work well in their classrooms all the time. There are two main reasons for this shift.

First, dramatic variations in students' abilities, cultures, languages, learning rates, and learning styles are forcing teachers to rethink their teaching. Homogeneous grouping can actually support segregation and exclusion of students that don't readily fit in for one reason or another. And today's classrooms have more and more of these hard-to-fit students. When homogeneous group teaching is the only strategy used, a few students might excel, naive learners might fall behind, and those with more significant disabilities might well end up barred from meaningful learning.

Second, evidence is growing that some learning is best accomplished when students learn together cooperatively, and that this type of learning often benefits all when group members bring different skills, information, and interests to a collective task. Such grouping is known as heterogeneous or mixed-ability grouping.

Teaching is almost never as simple as either/or. We encourage teachers to group students both ways—homogeneously and heterogeneously. In this chapter, we focus on providing guidelines and examples for teaching mixed-ability groups.

How Do Teachers Organize and Teach Mixed-Ability Groups?

Teaching heterogeneous groups requires a little more time to thoughtfully organize and plan for the groups' activities, at least at first. Let's start with two teachers' descriptions of how they used this type of grouping, shown in Figures 5.1 and 5.2.

Each example involves different students doing different activities. Yet successful learning in each case depends upon a common task and a set of effective strategies for organizing, planning, and teaching these groups. In this chapter, we identify three strategies, or "hints," for planning and teaching mixed-ability groups. We elaborate on each hint with three "tips" for helping ensure that the groups successfully accommodate and support students' learning differences. We group the hints and tips under three overall activities: organizing, planning, and teaching.

First, Organize

Remember, diversity is a strength, not a problem, if you can see it as an opportunity for creative

teaching and learning. Every student has something to offer and gain. The key to such teaching and learning is thoughtful selection of members for each group. Letting students choose their group mates is sometimes a good idea, but it does not guarantee heterogeneity. Teacher-selected groups, at least most of the time, give students an opportunity to work with and appreciate students different from themselves.

Educators experienced at organizing cooperative learning groups suggest a compromise between students selecting their own groups and teachers doing all the choosing. They recommend allowing students to name a few classmates they would most like to work with. Then teachers can organize groups with these preferences in mind. Revisiting students' preferences every few months or so encourages students to reflect on classmates they have gotten to know through teachers' grouping choices. Getting to know students through working together often creates new preferences for students.

Still, organizing groups is complicated because there are so many potential differences to consider. Our first hint and its accompanying tricks simplify this issue.

Hint 1: Maximize Variation Across Student Characteristics

Think about students' communication with classmates, their ways of behaving and the supports they might need, and their skills and abilities in relation to a group task. The most critical idea is balance—group students who are different from each other, then balance their differences. Also con-

5.1   A Teacher's Description of Teaching Heterogeneous Groups in 6th Grade

Transitioning from social studies to language arts halfway through my block class involves a 10-minute language warm-up activity (daily oral language). Using an overhead projector, I present three sentences with errors, one at a time. Groups of four to five students are sitting at each table. Each student has a role in a group. For example, at one table, Katie is the scribe, Brandon is the materials manager, Becky is the reader, and Maria monitors each member's participation.

After Becky reads the first sentence, Katie copies it into a notebook. All group members discuss possible errors. Brandon knows that all sentences should start with a capital letter, and he offers this advice. Maria adds that the sentence should have a period at the end. Becky explains the need for quotation marks, pointing out where Katie needs to add them to the sentence. Katie spots a word that should be changed to a plural and suggests this change to the group.

When students have finished correcting the first sentence, I display the next one. Discussion continues until all groups have corrected all three sentences. Each member contributes different levels of knowledge and assistance, but all are working on the same task.

I assemble my groups to encourage diversity. Students with stronger skills assist others, and the stronger learners' quick responses scaffold, or provide a foundation for learning, for students with fewer skills. In some cases, I can even overlap a student's specific learning objective. For example, Brandon is the materials manager because he needs to work on being better organized. Having the responsibility to organize, share, and generally keep track of the materials gives him important practice.

sider differences such as gender, age, cultural background, learning status (e.g., active learner, observer, methodical learner, and step-by-step learner), individual learning preferences and personalities, and physical and intellectual abilities. Although many differences can be considered, focusing on *communication, behavior,* and *skills* will help the most. Try to balance student abilities to communicate about the learning task and context, to do whatever the activity requires, and to cooperate with each other throughout the activity.

Communication refers to the ways in which students express themselves. Some students might be loud, bossy,

disrespectful, or interruptive and need other group members who can help them monitor their communication. Or students might be shy and reluctant to share their ideas at all and may need encouragement. Other students might communicate nonverbally, such as using sign language or electronic communication devices like a McCaw, or pointing to pictures.

Behavior refers to activities such as sitting and staying with a group, contributing to the organization and management of group work, paying attention to others as they participate, asking for help when it is needed, and interact-

5.2	A Teacher's Description of Teaching Heterogeneous Groups in High School

Along with my duties as a speech-language specialist, I coteach with Ms. Hayes in her high school reading class. She uses a reading fluency program called Read Naturally, a recent derivative of Marie Carbo's research-based Reading Styles Program. Because Read Naturally is specifically designed for students who read at a wide range of levels, students can work at their own pace and level. Groups of three to five students are seated at tables. Each group requires tape recorders, timers, and student notebooks. Students rotate three roles: The equipment manager gathers the recorders, timers, and notebooks; the timer listens to and times one-minute readings of group members; and the encourager makes sure that each member progresses and records progress on a data sheet.

Today starts with a whole-class vocabulary warm-up. The warm-up begins with the class brainstorming definitions and multiple meanings of words Ms. Hayes has selected from their readings.

Andrew offers the first definition for the word *strike*: "It's what I do in baseball."

Brenda asks, "Doesn't strike mean hit someone?"

Caleb adds, "My mom was on strike last summer when the workers tried to get pay raises."

Randy calls out, "You can bowl a strike."

After the group brainstorms meanings for a couple of words, the lesson shifts to following the Read Naturally procedures for the next 30 minutes.

At one table, Ray is listening through earphones to a story tape as he reads along in his Level 2.5 story packet. Ruth, who is working on Level 7.0, is timing Pam, as Pam performs her final oral reading on her Level 6.0 passage. After completing the reading portion of his Level 3.5 story, Brian is engrossed in an intricate illustration that he is including as part of his story retell. The group continues to work through the 10-step reading/retell process. Each group member ends the session by recording daily progress on individualized graphs in their notebooks.

I keep the groups fairly small so I can balance different students' strengths and weaknesses with other students who can complement them. I rotate the roles to make sure that all students are contributing and feel equally valued. Each role is doable for all students, though occasionally I have noticed that members of a group may support a peer who is finding a role difficult.

ing with the other group members.

Skills refers to the varying degrees of depth and mastery students bring to any learning situation. Some students may already be familiar with the content and tasks, using a particular lesson to refresh and maintain their ability and information or to expand upon a strength. Other students equally familiar with the lesson's content and tasks may expand and deepen their mastery by exploring related ideas, helping other students learn, or serving as a leader of the group's efforts. Students may be just learning the basic concepts and skills, often requiring more teaching support and assistance during these early stages of learning acquisition. Some students may be somewhat familiar with the content and tasks, but need more practice with the ideas to become fluent with using them. There may also be students participating in a group activity to learn only some of the content and skills.

Skills may include a student's ability to contribute to others' learning not specifically related to a task. For example, if the specific content of a group task is familiar to a student, and he is also skillful in explaining what he knows to classmates, he might be able to support someone who is working on acquiring the basic concepts. In the process of teaching, he deepens his own learning. The familiar aphorism, "The best way to learn is to try to teach," works for learning at all ages.

In general, try to organize your mixed-ability groups so that each student's strengths and weaknesses balance those of the others in the group. To illustrate Hint 1, we describe two heterogeneous groups in Figure 5.3, on page 78.

Tip 1: Balance Teaching Attention Across the Day and Week

Teachers often create groups of similar learners so they can teach all of them at once. Same-ability grouping practices assume that each student receives an equal amount of teaching attention. If someone in the group needs a different kind of teaching assistance, others have to wait, or the student has to wait until the teacher finishes with the rest of the group. This sequential approach—trying to give everyone a fair share of attention during each lesson—often results in many group members having down time, when they are not learning anything at all.

When groups of diverse learners are balanced to complement different levels of communications, behavior, and abilities, some students in the group actually need less teaching attention than others. Students who are practicing or maintaining previously acquired information and skills need less direct teaching than those who are working on mastering basic concepts and skills. From a teacher's point of view, groups of diverse learners should always include some who need less teacher attention and some who require more. Low-intensity learners in one group, however, might be higher-intensity learners in another group.

Instead of trying to balance teaching attention evenly within each lesson, teachers use mixed-ability groups to help them balance their teaching attention for any particular student across the day and week. When students are not receiving focused teaching attention, they might be learning from or teaching a peer, practicing already learned skills, or exploring a topic in more depth by leading a group's activity.

Ask yourself these questions to help you balance your attention across students:

• Do I want to spend time paying focused attention to every student across all curricular areas each week?

• Can I describe, at least every two weeks, how well any student is learning in all key areas?

• Do the students I find challenging have

daily learning experiences they find positive and successful?

• Do the students I find quick-and-easy learners have daily learning experiences they find challenging and rewarding?

• Do all my students have the opportunity to learn from other adults, peers, and students in this school? Can I describe these opportunities?

Tip 2: Balance Students' Roles Within a Group

Organizing groups so that students serve different roles is another way to maximize diversity of key student characteristics. The examples from Ms. Clark and Ms. Jackson (Figure 5.3) illustrate how these teachers organized their groups so that the efforts of each member were needed by the group.

It's also a good idea to mix enthusiastic with more reluctant learners when possible. Make sure that every group has at least one student who can serve as a model of cooperation and consideration for others. Conversely, make sure that no group has more than one student who requires much support and guidance to behave well.

To avoid the pitfall of a group with several leaders and no followers, try not to group several students with assertive personalities together. Grouping too many quiet, passive students may result in too little leadership, leaving the group rudderless and drifting. If an activity demands different kinds of abilities at different points— such as good writing and artwork to create products like the Egypt travel brochures in Ms. Clark's class—try to organize groups where different students can contribute their special competence and

also benefit from others' unique abilities.

Make sure that groups with students who require physical assistance also include at least one student who enjoys helping. Students needing special devices to communicate, write, or sit properly can be assisted by other group members who are fascinated by these aids and willing to wait instead of speaking or moving for their less physically able peers.

Ask yourself these questions to help balance student roles in groups:

• Do groups have a good mix of leaders and followers?

• Do groups have someone who can serve as a good model for cooperation, interest, and behavior?

• Do groups have members with special talents for important parts of this activity?

• Do groups have someone to support or assist others who need it?

• Do groups have a good mix of working paces among the students, so that the group works neither too fast nor too slowly for any one student?

Tip 3: Balance Teaching Locations, Formats, and Materials

Working with mixed-ability groups offers many opportunities for creativity. Teachers can use different locations for learning: other parts of the school, the community, businesses and community services, other teachers' classrooms, and so on. Teaching formats and materials allow almost as much range, from group investigations using photo albums and memorabilia brought

5.3   Examples of Teaching Heterogeneous Groups

From Ms. Clark, a 6th Grade General Education Teacher

Ms. Hendricks and I share an educational assistant, Ms. Dean. Three times a week, Ms. Dean assists me in the writer's workshop portion of my social studies/language arts block. Writer's workshop involves many different activities occurring simultaneously. I chose the student groups, trying to balance students' strengths and weaknesses across both their current mastery of this task and other important group characteristics, such as getting along with each other and working well together.

The social studies portion of the block we had just completed was a unit on Egypt. Today's writer's workshop requires students to design, illustrate, and write a travel brochure for Egypt. One group includes Brandon, a reluctant writer who often has difficulty expressing himself with words. But he is a terrific artist. Becky, who is at the top of the class in spelling and punctuation but limited in her creativity, joins him. Bill will also work in this group. His family has traveled extensively, and he is an inspired writer, bringing a tremendous amount of background knowledge to the group. Susannah will work with this group, along with Audrey, who is loaded down with magazines and catalogs for Susannah. Audrey plans to help Susannah cut out and paste pictures for her brochure.

A second group is using the Inspiration program on the computers. This program helps students organize information by creating a variety of webs and maps with choices from different graphics and text. Josiah, who has trouble sitting still and focusing for more than a few minutes at a time, is sitting beside Tasha. Tasha, an unflappable and accomplished writer, is concentrating on an intricate web of graphics and text. Katie, seated on the other side of Tasha, is seldom excited about learning and has trouble focusing. But today, she is engrossed in the wide array of colorful graphics displayed on her partially completed brochure cover. She is sitting next to Eli, who interrupts her often for help with the text portion of his project. When Josiah begins to get distracted and vocal, group members either ignore him or offer suggestions for his project. Ms. Dean and I stop by this group often to monitor progress.

From Ms. Jackson, an Elementary-Level, Speech-Language Specialist

On Tuesdays and Thursdays, I go to Spruce Elementary School to check in with the students and classrooms designated as needing language supports. Ms. Thompson, the school's reading specialist, joins

---

me, and together we work with Mr. White's 1st grade class during reading. His class is working on phonological awareness or sound discrimination skills. Four students have IEP goals for language or reading. Another student has limited English skills.

This morning, Mr. White's class is seated on the floor, gathered around their teacher as he teaches them a new rhyming poem. There's a lot of excitement when Ms. Thompson and I arrive. The students bounce up and down, raising their hands to be chosen for the three proposed games they'll be playing in different parts of the classroom. I select a group of six students, including three with IEP language goals. One of the three also speaks limited English. I have chosen a Bingo game that uses pictures of items found around a home instead of letters and numbers.

Before starting the game, the group discusses the pictures on the Bingo cards, randomly choosing pictures of items to identify beginning sounds. Tanya begins the game by choosing a game piece with a picture of a sink. She is able to name the picture and tell the group the beginning sound as members search their Bingo cards for a sink.

Alfonso is next, and he chooses a picture of a chair. He labels chair in Spanish. I ask him if he can tell the group in English. He quietly replies, labeling the chair in English. The group is asked to identify the beginning sound in *chair*.

Caleb's turn is next. He chooses a picture of a bed, identifies the beginning sound, and shares that *bed* rhymes with *head*. His rhyme inspires the group to rhyme with the two pieces chosen earlier.

Brandy chooses a picture of a telephone. She quickly identifies the beginning sound and proceeds to clap the number of syllables/sounds in the word. The game continues for the next 20 minutes, with the students practicing a range of sound discrimination and language skills.

Although the students may think I chose the group randomly, the group's makeup actually reinforces different skills for individual students. Tanya has an objective on her IEP targeting the discrimination of initial sounds in words. Alfonso's IEP includes labeling common objects. Caleb's IEP objectives include learning the range of phonological awareness skills, such as rhyme, and identifying sounds in different positions of words. The remaining students in the group are working on the current classroom curriculum objective of counting syllables in words. With different levels of prompting, all students practice an array of language skills.

from home, to computer and video technology.

Remember to balance choices of teaching locations, formats, and materials for any particular group session, making sure that the choices are compatible. For example, group members engaged in a problem-solving discussion while other members are trying to work individually may be distracting and unwieldy, slowing everyone's learning. If some students are working with modeling clay and paints, other group members who are trying to write final copy for their books may have trouble concentrating.

The point is to try to make sure that when students have different roles in a group, are working on mastering tasks in different ways, and perhaps even working on different learning objectives, the learning locations, formats, and materials have some commonality.

Then, Plan

Organizing well-balanced and diverse groups of learners is only the first step in effective mixed-ability group teaching. You also need to plan carefully how students will use group time to learn well and efficiently. Fortunately, the days of individual worksheets and reports, group drill, and recitation of memorized facts are gradually disappearing. Teaching and learning look and sound different in classrooms that are using cooperative and transactional approaches. Such approaches help ensure that all students not only learn information that makes sense to them, but also use that learning in their lives outside school.

Two phrases seem to characterize these emerging approaches to teaching and learning: messiness and shared responsibility. Let's look at each in detail.

Messiness

Lessons and classrooms look and sound messier. Students are talking and working together in groups of all sizes. Desks, chairs, and materials are organized to aid the work of students rather than the cleaning of floors. More activity is evident during the day, or even during a single lesson. Students seem to move around more and change their minds about what to do next, as learning takes new and unexpected turns. The effect is productive disorder. Teachers are everywhere, not just at the front of the room. Sometimes you can't even tell if there *is* a front of the room.

Shared Responsibility

Students take more responsibility for deciding not only what to learn, but also how it is learned. Teachers negotiate with students, both individually and in groups, about the work they are doing, the quality that must be achieved, and the time frames within which work is completed. One important aspect of cooperative learning is that students must share responsibility for each others' learning, nurturing others' strengths and accommodating their weaknesses. Teaching and learning are increasingly alive, sometimes unpredictable, and almost always more fun for everybody. Students may learn different things, but still things that matter to them. At the same time, they are acquiring habits of caring, imagining, thinking, understanding, empathizing, being humble, and enjoying their learning. In short, they become responsible members of the social group.

Despite their messiness, teaching and learning that achieve both competence and social responsibility work best when carefully planned. Hint 2 summarizes the focus of this planning.

Hint 2: Maximize Positive Interdependence

Good planning results in positive interdependence, when students develop relationships with each other, learn to depend upon and respect each other, and figure out how to negotiate and resolve differences that arise. Interdependence involves cooperation, community, and consensus. Planning can aid or hinder achieving this kind of cohesive working climate. Structure a lesson so that all group members perceive all other members as needed. Arrange for students who are less able, or perhaps less well-liked because of an annoying characteristic or behavior, to have some expertise that the group needs to accomplish its task. Ms. Clark's description of how she used literature circles midway through the year exemplifies the different levels of learning that can occur (Figure 5.4, page 82).

Tip 1: Plan Teaching Content That Is Related and Valued

One advantage to mixed-ability group teaching and learning is that all students in a group do not have to be learning the same thing at the

same time. In the literature circle example, students are working on slightly different learning objectives, each related to reading, understanding, connecting, and analyzing. Some students are learning discrete parts of a task, such as communication or English skills. Some are learning how to coordinate group efforts to reach a high standard of quality. Others are working on learning objectives related to comprehension, reading fluency, vocabulary, and perspective taking.

Ask yourself these questions to plan related and valued teaching content:

- Are students' individual learning tasks related or complementary?
- Do students' individual learning tasks take compatible amounts of time to complete, both in general and with regard to the other students' work pace?
- Is the location for the lesson a reasonably natural setting, given the activity and tasks?
- Are the materials and logistics for using the materials related and compatible?

Tip 2: Script the Flow

Supporting each group member takes planning. Some will need brief encouragement; some, quick feedback and correction; and some, praise. Even though your teaching attention may be focused on one or two members of each group, or maybe even just one or two of all the groups in your class that day, your praise, encouragement, support, and feedback to all ensure active participation.

Keep in mind, too, that more cooperative group learning also allows some of this balance

5.4   Using Literature Circles to Promote Interdependence

From Ms. Clark, a 6th Grade General Education Teacher

I have experimented with ways to increase student discussion around literature ever since the state came out with its reading benchmarks. Asking kids questions in the three test areas of comprehension, extensions, and analysis in literature logs was getting some results, but many of the kids in my class do not *like* to write, or cannot manage their time well enough to accomplish more than a token response. I would often go home with a stack of journals that told me nothing. When Mr. West, our librarian, told me about literature circles and the possibilities of 6th grade students actually talking about books the way adult book groups do, I decided to give it a try. What I liked was the opportunities for book choices to be student driven, for children to manage a book within an allotted amount of time, and for each child to have a role and a responsibility to take to the circle.

Literature circles involve groups of three to five kids who agree to read a book and meet several times a week to discuss what they've read. I introduced the idea to the class over a two-week period, teaching them each of the five main roles (described in Chapter 1) separately. We worked on "fat" questions (questions that require complex and analytical thinking) and "skinny" questions (questions that require yes, no, or single-word responses). These were hard concepts for many students. They wanted to ask questions like, "What color was the main character's house?" rather than, "Who does the main character remind you of?"

Mr. West gave us a talk about several books in the library on the day the students were to choose their books. They voted by secret ballot for their first three choices. It was amazingly easy to give all the kids their first or second choice and to group them heterogeneously. Excited, we were ready to start the next day.

Later, I would have to make a frantic call to another school doing literature circles to make sure the feelings of frustration I was having were normal. Eli read, but never quite got his role sheet, which assigned him a thinking task related to his role, completed on time. Mark had trouble keeping up. Becky was ready to finish her book in a night.

But we stayed with it! The students used books on tape, teacher reading, or peer reading, and they buddied-up and began to assign themselves homework. Fast readers made sure they followed the circle plan and came to the circle ready to discuss only the assigned pages. Each meeting was a tiny bit better. Darren and I had a standing date to read *Maniac Magee*. Josh checked with his support study hall teacher to plump up his "fat" questions when he was the discussion director.

5.4 Using Literature Circles to Promote Interdependence—*continued*

After two weeks, I surveyed the groups for pluses and minuses and learned they were struggling with plain old group dynamics. We are still working on the "person who fools around" and the "people who don't do their work."

We had a little celebration when we finished the first books. Each child gave a final response or reaction to their reading, and each group spent three reading class periods making a response project. The projects included mobiles, totem poles, artwork, and other three-dimensional representations of their reading. We invited Mr. West to watch as each group stood and talked about their book. Eli had read *Jeremy Thatcher Dragon Hatcher* and had worked on an elaborate clay model diorama. Maria, with her *Where the Red Fern Grows* group, proudly talked about how she had cried at the end of the story and had never cried about a story before. Every kid spoke, and sometimes they prompted each other to remember.

I am not yet sure literature circles will work, but I know my students have been caught talking about books outside the circles. I found out that Maria had already started *The Giver*. And one group of three came and asked me if they could have a secret literature circle.

to be achieved by students' interactions with each other as well as with you. When your attention is focused on the students or the groups you have targeted for more intense teaching, other group members and other groups can praise, encourage, support, and provide feedback to each other.

Assigning cooperative group roles is one technique that teachers find naturally encourages this kind of balance between student and teacher interactions for all group members. It can also teach students to work with everyone in a group and to learn about themselves as they learn about other students. One way to teach collaborative skills to a student who has trouble listening or who sometimes disrupts the group is

to have that student observe and collect data on other students' turn taking. Another strategy is to have the student assume the role of encourager, with the assignment of praising others' listening and cooperation.

Try to picture in your mind what the sequence of events is, how each student participates, how you interact with students, and how they interact with each other. Ask yourself these questions to help balance teacher-student and student-student interactions:

• Does each student interact with all the other group members for various purposes and at various times during the lesson or activity?

• Do you interact with every student in the

groups you are focusing on?

• Do you find a way to be in touch with those groups you are not focusing on sometime during the lesson or activity?

• Are all the students in each group engaged for the entire lesson or activity, or do some students experience down time?

Tip 3: Encourage Group Cooperation and Problem Solving

As discussed earlier, balancing teaching locations, formats, and materials offers opportunities for creativity. You are free to plan the use of those materials and the sequence of tasks to foster interdependence among group members.

Make sure students are physically close to each other. Facing each other across a table or sitting in a small close circle of chairs fosters more interaction and cooperation than when desks are spread out. Be creative about how students organize themselves for work. Sitting on the floor in a corner, huddling around one student's chair, and lying on the floor with heads together are all possible ways of being physically close enough to work together.

How you choose to organize materials and tasks can also promote group cooperation and problem solving. Making only one set of materials for each group forces members to share, just as creating a single group product forces students to collaborate and problem-solve. Sometimes different students have different parts of the materials or information resources, requiring the group to figure out how to use each other to complete the task. For example, assigning group members different roles and

responsibilities in the literature circle ensured that discussions occurred as planned and that everyone contributed. Organizing the group project at the end of each book so that each student's work was necessary to complete the entire task is another example.

Ask yourself these questions to help arrange students, tasks, and materials:

• Do students have everything they need readily at hand?

• Does the group waste time moving about unnecessarily to complete tasks or get needed materials?

• Do group members manage tasks and materials cooperatively and actively problem-solve difficulties or conflicts?

• Do groups work efficiently and productively?

Maximizing positive interdependence involves helping students build the relationships and shared experiences with each other that result in a sense of community and shared learning. Membership in these communities of learning supports students outside school as they try to become participating, contributory members of the broader community.

Finally, Teach!

Once you have organized groups to maximize diversity, organized tasks and materials so they are compatible, and planned the flow of the group lesson to maximize students' interdependence, it is time to teach! Of course, you cannot always be present in every group. But your careful planning will have targeted certain groups for your focused teaching attention while others receive your more intermittent, but equally important, support and feedback. Our third hint focuses on the point of all your organizing, planning, and movement among groups and offers three tips for achieving this point.

Hint 3: Maximize Student Learning by Using Effective Teaching Strategies

We assume that you are a good teacher, and we know that even good teachers sometimes need their thinking about teaching and learning validated. If you haven't refreshed your ideas about teaching and learning for a while, we have included a list of resources at the end of this chapter that might help you renew your vision and practice. We encourage you to pick one of the selections and take some time to confirm and expand your reflections about this aspect of your work.

Your role as a teacher is to watch what students are doing, figure out why they are doing it that way, and then give them the right kind and amount of information so that they can do what you are teaching them to do without you. Learning doesn't always mean getting the right answer or doing something the right way. More than being right, learning involves knowing what the learning means and how it fits into students' experiences, both inside and outside school. Students must be able to make sense of what is taught if they are going to use it.

Tip 1: Give Help Based on Students' Performance

Two of the most important components of good teaching are giving students help and giving them feedback. Knowing how to help students first requires both you and the students to be clear about what you want them to do. Help also involves knowing how much and what kind of assistance to give students before a task, so that they are able to discover for themselves the best way to do it. Just telling students what to do, or giving them one way to do something, is often not useful. Figuring out how to help students requires moment-to-moment decisions. Sometimes you'll tell them what to notice that might give them clues about what to do. Sometimes it's better to point, nod, or use a facial expression or other gesture. Showing students something or even physically helping them the first time they try a task may be what's needed.

Whatever combination of support you provide, remember that what you do is beneficial if, as a result of your efforts, the student performs well and knows why she was successful. Good teaching always focuses on what the student is doing and thinking.

Good teaching also involves noting and rewarding both individual and group achievements. Praising correct responses and bringing individual achievements to the attention of other group members are examples of positive and supportive feedback. You can also encourage students' support of each other. Often peer feedback is a more powerful way to motivate and achieve learning.

Sometimes, your feedback needs to be corrective. Even well-designed help doesn't always eliminate student mistakes. Positive corrective feedback focuses not so much on getting a student to stop doing something wrong as on trying to help the student understand his mistakes so that he can avoid them in the future. Before giving corrective feedback, first analyze students' mistakes. Different kinds of mistakes require different kinds of help, so make sure that you accurately understand the mistakes made. The best kind of corrective feedback is teaching help offered before the student's next attempt. In Figure 5.5, Ms. Jackson talks about how she gave feedback to Cara, a nonverbal 2nd grade student who requires communication support.

Providing this kind of individual help and feedback is critical, but unless the groups have been organized to maximize diversity and you have been teaching students to support each other's learning, it can be challenging to manage. Consider an example from Ms. Clark's class, shown in Figure 5.6. She describes feedback between students.

Ask yourself these questions to learn about your students' individual learning experiences:

• Do students receive help from each other as well as from you?
• If a student seems to be acquiring new skills and information unusually slowly, is it because the student is getting too much of the wrong kind of help?
• Are any students beginning to depend upon help before they even try parts of a task?
• Do all students receive the help they need

to "get it right" in ways that are not noticeable or intrusive to the group?
• What kinds of mistakes are students making and why?
• What can be different about student feedback or help that will minimize students' mistakes?
• Do students feel supported and rewarded when they perform well?

Tip 2: Clarify Expectations and "Check in" on Student Behavior

Even though you may be targeting only one or two groups for your focused teaching attention, as orchestrator of all groups, you must make sure that they stay on task and finish within established time lines. Group work is messier and noisier than individual work, but it still must occur within reasonable parameters of noise and disorder.

Many students need to systematically learn how to be good group members. Much of their schooling may have previously emphasized largely independent work. Learning to wait for a turn, not interrupt others, share materials and ideas, stay with the group, ask for help, support other members' learning, and pay attention when a member needs more time to work out part of an activity may be new and unfamiliar to them. Some teachers find that a class may take weeks or even months to learn how to work well in groups. Two strategies that help this process are making sure you lead group openings and closures and checking in on behavior.

Most teachers set up group tasks by explaining what will happen to all the groups together.

5.5	Example of Feedback from a Teacher to a Student

Cara is often frustrated by her inability to articulate her wants, needs, thoughts, and opinions. She often resorts to physical communication, pushing or grabbing at her peers, resulting in problems with peer relationships. Cara misses much school because of illnesses and family dysfunction. She uses a limited communication board at school, but she often forgets or misplaces it between home and school. Her communication board includes pictures of items important to Cara, along with concepts such as "I want" and "I need," and has voice output, so that when she presses a picture, the voice expresses for Cara what she wants to say.

Today, Cara is in tears after an episode on the playground. A recess monitor reprimanded her for grabbing a jump rope from another student. Cara is trying to communicate her side of the story with a combination of gestures and sign language (in which she is not yet fluent). I ask her to use her communication board. She shakes her head, indicating that she doesn't know where it is. She is at a loss for a way to communicate. I restate my interpretation of her dilemma, and she nods her head in affirmation. We begin to work on a series of picture cards showing the concepts of "please" and "I want." Then we draw a series of items found on the playground, such as a ball, jump rope, swing, and monkey bars. I explain that she is to ask her friends for recess items by showing them the cards or pointing. We call in her friend, Karen, to help us practice. I ask Cara where we can keep the cards, and she indicates in her pocket. We compromise by encasing them in plastic, punching a hole, and attaching them to a belt loop with a big key ring.

The next day I observe Cara at recess. She begins to reach for a ball as another student is bouncing it. I quickly step in and point to her key ring. Cara stops. She finds her pictures of "please" and "ball" and shows them to the other student, who then offers to play with her. Success! Cara has initiated a positive interaction with a peer.

Try to make sure that these openings also include a review of rules for group work. Some teachers even use the first group activities to create rules needed for effective learning. Even though students within a group might be learning different knowledge, this review of common group process can remind them about the cohesive and collaborative nature of effective learning groups.

Similarly, it is wise to end groups together. Group reports are one way to have closure. Often the content of these reports is the groups' tasks, but closure might also include reports on some aspects of group management, such as how the group felt everyone contributed or which members seemed to be especially deserving of praise for their work.

5.6	Example of Feedback from One Student to Another

Mark missed most of the fall term because of a critical illness in his family. He was supposed to be attending school in the city his family had traveled to for the medical help they needed. He returned to my 6th grade classroom, after missing a half-year of bonding and growing with his classmates.

I tried to encourage him to get back on track, but Mark would tattle on his classmates and some days tell me he "just felt bad." When I pushed him to make journal entries, he wrote me apologies and told me he'd do better, but he didn't do his work. Perhaps he was feeling a little neglected at home, with so much time spent on his gravely ill brother. I could only guess.

When we formed literature circles, Mark chose *Where the Red Fern Grows*. He was in a group with Bill, a wonderful, motivated student; Jill, a middle-of-the-road plugger; Audrey, a good reader and fair worker; and Becky, a troubled young lady with above-average reading skills. I knew the group would be a challenge. They had a rocky start, but as the literature circle became routine, the group seemed to be trying. They "reported" on each other, and Becky bossed them unmercifully on some days.

I thought Bill would step up to take charge, but Mark was the one. Mark loved the book. I sat in on the group discussion one day when Mark was the "literary luminary." His job was to highlight passages that were meaningful in some way: funny, interesting, or descriptive. He had the group turn to a particular page and paragraph and asked Audrey to read a passage aloud. In the story, Billy was talking about looking into Little Anne's eyes and the connection they had. When Audrey was finished, Mark explained that he had picked this passage because it reminded him of his brother. He said that he could look into his brother's eyes, and even though his brother said he was feeling okay, Mark could tell by his eyes that he was not.

Later, when we had a short debriefing session, Becky spoke up and openly complimented Mark. I used his example other times as a positive illustration of a student who wasn't doing well initially, but was able to connect with the story and positively influence the group. Now it's Mark who urges the group to stay on task and get their jobs done. He still writes me apologies, but he's also looking forward to reading the next book.

After reminding students of your rules for effective collaboration, you can then manage the ongoing work of the groups by checking in on students' behavior and using good examples to counter less desirable performance. Most teachers are masterful users of behavior checks. The piercing look to a student who is starting to talk to a classmate instead of listening to a student reading his theme is an example. Another strategy is praising one student's behavior to counter his neighbor's misbehavior.

These strategies for coaxing good student behavior are effective both in small learning groups and with a whole class. If you have reviewed working rules as part of your opening, then they can become the substance of your ongoing behavior checks.

Ask yourself these questions to learn how groups are functioning:

• Are all the groups working productively and efficiently?

• Are students helping each other instead of waiting for you?

• Are students figuring out how to enrich and enhance their learning without your guidance at least some of the time?

• Do students' work outcomes and products sometimes surprise you?

• Do students figure out how to incorporate all students without your help, including those who are less motivated, have learning limitations, or pose other challenges to the group's work and climate?

• Do students make unprompted suggestions for further learning experiences and tasks?

Tip 3: Collect Student Performance Information

If students learn what you are attempting to teach them, then they can move on to continue their learning. If they are not learning, you probably will want to change your teaching plan. Successful teaching and learning don't happen for all students unless teachers have all the information they need about each student. We have found that many teachers struggle with how

much and what kind of student performance data to collect.

First, collect only the information you need to make the changes in students' learning experiences so that you can assure effective and timely progress. Second, be as creative as possible about how you collect the information.

Ask yourself these questions about collecting student performance information and changing your teaching:

• What information do I need to convince me that each student is learning?

• Can I get this information in some simple, unobtrusive way?

• Can the students themselves collect this information for me?

• Am I reviewing information about student learning daily? Weekly? Often enough so that students' learning is not slowing down and they are not practicing mistakes or learning misrules?

• Am I making changes in my teaching and in students' learning experiences that result in better student performance?

As valuable as teaching mixed-ability groups can be, its success must be measured in terms of growth in individual student competence. We discuss methods for measuring individual competence in mixed-ability groups in Chapter 6.

Tools for Reflective Teaching

We offer two tools to help you think divergently about your efforts. The first is a list of questions to ask yourself throughout the day about your teaching generally and about a particular lesson or activity. Figure 5.7 shows the questions. We originally created this list as a bookmark, but it could also be used as a poster—or whatever means might help keep it handy. The second tool is a journal page for daily, ongoing reflection about your teaching. Figure 5.8 shows an example. Some teachers keep a journal on their computer. Others write their ideas on an index card that they can file for review when they are planning new lessons or units.

5.7	Questions for Teachers to Ask Themselves Daily

About my teaching in general

1. What did I learn today about each student's ability? Competence?
2. What did I learn today about how each student learns best?
3. Are my students interested and having fun in their learning?
4. Are they learning knowledge that matters to them? How do I know?
5. Are they using knowledge they learn in my class outside my class? How do I know?
6. Are my students positive toward each other?
7. What changes do I have to make? What do I want to do tomorrow?
8. Am I having fun yet?

When working with students

1. Are students doing what I planned? Why or why not?
2. Are students working consistently and productively? Why or why not?
3. Are any students confused? Why? What am I going to do about it?
4. How can I improve my teaching plan? Would changes in the following areas help students learn more effectively?

- Lesson or task design.
- Physical context.
- Presentation and design of materials.
- Timing or pacing of the lesson or activity.
- Student feedback.
- Student choices.
- Student communication and collaboration.

5. What would make the biggest difference and give me the most useful information? How will I know?

6. Is there anything I should remember to do from the start next time?

5.8	Example of a Teacher's Reflective Journal Page

Date: *Tuesday, March 16*

What did I teach today?
- *Queen Hattie*
- *Reading from the textbook.*
- *Students compiled lists of ceremonial garb.*

What went well and why?
- *Nadine and Tasha worked well together for reading (Tasha was very patient).*
- *Most were able to compile lists independently when given the choice of graphics or words.*

What do I need to change and how?
- *Peer assistant (Samuel) is not a good match with Josh, Brandon, Maria, and Jamie. Try Anna as assistant next time for reading.*
- *Try a picture sequence schedule for creating a list for Susannah next time to increase independence.*

Notes and reminders:
- *When it's time to draw Hattie, make a picture available for students who are uncomfortable with drawing or who cannot draw.*
- *Make sure students have their vocabulary/concept webs with them to help create their lists and check to see if they've left anything out.*
- *Ask Anna if she can assist on Thursday.*

For Further Reading

Creating a positive and welcoming school climate is a first step in developing successful learning environments. The following resources may help you think about strategies for classroom management, behavior support, and fostering a positive school climate: Armstrong (2000); DiGiuilio (2000); Epstein, Kutash, and Duchnowski (1998); Harlan and Rowland (1999); Kohn (1996a); and Repp and Horner (1999).

Cooperative learning strategies have been helpful to many teachers in organizing classrooms to promote constructive social dynamics and interpersonal development. As starting points to understand why, see Johnson and Johnson (1999); Johnson, Johnson, and Holubec (1995); Putnam (1998); Slavin (1999); and Topping and Ehly (1998). The resources by Kohn (1996b), Office of Special Education Programs (2000), and Freiberg (1998) look specifically at how classrooms and schools might be structured to foster inclusive education in a positive climate.

Armstrong, T. (2000). *ADD/ADHD alternatives in the classroom.* Alexandria, VA: Association for Supervision and Curriculum Development.

DiGiuilio, R. (2000). *Positive classroom management. A step-by-step guide to successfully running the show without destroying student dignity* (2nd ed.). Thousand Oaks, CA: Corwin Press, Inc.

Epstein, M. H., Kutash, K., & Duchnowski, A. (Eds.). (1998). *Outcomes for children and youth with emotional and behavioral disorders and their families: Programs and evaluation best practices.* Austin, TX: Pro-Ed., Inc.

Freiberg, H. J. (1998). Measuring school climate: Let me count the ways. *Educational Leadership, 56*(1), 22–26.

Harlan, J. C., & Rowland, S. T. (1999). *Behavior management strategies for teachers. A student workbook.* Springfield, IL: Charles C. Thomas Publisher, Ltd.

Johnson, D. W., & Johnson, R. T. (1999). Making cooperative learning work. *Theory into Practice, 38*(2), 67–73.

Johnson, D. W., Johnson, R. T., & Holubec, E. J. (1995). *Cooperative learning in the classroom.* Alexandria, VA: Association for Supervision and Curriculum Development.

Kohn, A. (1996a). *Beyond discipline: From compliance to community.* Alexandria, VA: Association for Supervision and Curriculum Development.

Kohn, A. (1996b). What to look for in a classroom. *Educational Leadership, 54*(1), 54–55.

Office of Special Education Programs. (2000). *Improving education: The promise of inclusive schooling.* Denver, CO: National Institute for Urban Education.

Putnam, J. W. (Ed.). (1998). *Cooperative learning and strategies for inclusion: Celebrating diversity in the classroom* (2nd ed.). Baltimore, MD: Paul H. Brookes Publishing Co.

Repp, A. C., & Horner, R. H. (1999). *Functional analysis of problem behavior: From effective assessment to effective support.* Belmont, CA: Wadsworth Publishing Co.

Slavin, R. E. (1999). Comprehensive approaches to cooperative learning. *Theory into Practice, 38*(2), 74–79.

Topping, K., & Ehly, S. (Eds.). (1998). *Peer-assisted learning.* Mahwah, NJ: Lawrence Erlbaum Associates.

Recommended Web Sites

http://nrsi.com/ The National Reading Styles Institute (NRSI) is a research-based educational organization dedicated to improving literacy. NRSI employs the services of an extensive network of consultants and trainers throughout the United States. Some consultants work exclusively with the institute, but many are working principals, staff developers, teachers, curriculum coordinators, directors, and superintendents.

http://www.nrsi.com/askmarie/askmarie2.html. The Carbo Reading Styles Program is a proven, effective approach to changing reading instruction that begins at the classroom level, honors what we know about how both young people and teachers learn best, and is grounded in practicality and 20 years of solid research.

Ongoing Recording and Reporting

This chapter discusses collecting student learning and performance data to help teachers make curriculum and teaching decisions. We've chosen this emphasis because all too often, using performance data to make such decisions is overshadowed by the need to use it to satisfy external demands for program accountability.

The Current Assessment Climate

Figuring out what students know and can do is a complex and controversial topic. When U.S. schools focused primarily on teaching facts and skills, assessing what students knew seemed more straightforward. We are all familiar with the ever-present achievement test—a reasonably efficient and inexpensive way of finding out what large numbers of students remember (at least until the test is over).

As the focus has shifted from content-centered instruction to a growing interest in how children and youth apply their learning to their lives, the usefulness of the traditional achievement test has diminished. Educators now discuss and debate ways to assess student performance in novel situations. They are increasingly interested in finding out what students know and can do with what students have been taught, rather than how students answer standardized test questions that may have little relevance to what they were taught or learned. Educators are also interested in students acquiring a better understanding of their own learning, so that they might continue to pursue their education long after formal schooling ends.

Schools are currently emphasizing that students learn *certain* things to a *certain* degree of proficiency or performance. This standards-based approach, or movement, as it is frequently called, makes good sense in some ways. We should have the same high expectations for learning and achievement for *all* children and youth, especially those for whom our system of education has frequently held lower expectations—such as students with disabilities, students from certain ethnic groups, and students who come from lower-income and challenging family situations.

The standards-based movement, however, can be problematic for teachers and their students. First, if the standards are expressed as discrete bits of information or narrow skills, creating cooperative, integrated, project-based learning activities that address each discrete skill or fact can be difficult. Teachers feel more secure directly teaching each fact or skill—teaching to the test. Although this strategy helps ensure that students acquire the facts and skills, it can compromise students' interest and motivation for learning, as well as use of their learning. Students may not be able to figure out how to apply facts or skills that have been learned outside of meaningful and relevant contexts. Teachers who must teach to narrowly articulated standards have to work harder to weave them into thematic units of integrated curriculum and to develop the strategies to monitor what has and has not been addressed.

Discrete standards are also harder for students to meet in different ways and to varying degrees. Classrooms can quickly become standardized in their approach to learning, rather than individually tailored. When standards are broadly framed, teachers can address them within the context of units like "Egypt" and tailor meeting the standards to the abilities and purposes of each student.

A second way standards-based reforms might be problematic is the degree to which the standards are high stakes. If promotion to the next grade or receiving a diploma depends on meeting standards, once again, teachers may be encouraged to teach to the standards. Such efforts homogenize teaching and learning and limit possibilities for individual tailoring. Homogenization of teaching may also occur if teachers' contracts or merit pay increases are tied to the number or proportion of students who meet the standards.

Discussions about assessment, testing, achievement, standards, and effective schools represent a large body of literature. To develop authentic approaches to learning and to communicate what their students know and can do as a result of schooling, teachers are experimenting with new strategies for collecting information about student learning. They are becoming more confident that they can design curriculum and learning activities that incorporate a wide range of student diversity. But they are less clear about how innovations for documenting student learning and performance can be used with all students.

In this chapter, we first offer a framework for teachers to document student learning. Then we discuss how new strategies for collecting this information can fit into the framework. Finally, we describe two tools, the ITER and the ITER

Summary, for collecting and documenting learning for students who are difficult to gather information about—students for whom conventional strategies are neither informative nor possible. Often, these are students with disabilities, children with cultural or linguistic differences, or students who are able and quick learners.

A Big Picture Framework

The framework organizes information about learning gain and performance from a classroom teacher's point of view. As stated earlier, we choose to emphasize using student learning and performance information to make curriculum and teaching decisions. Teachers need individually tailored classroom-based assessment systems that first and foremost help them maximize student learning. These systems need to be simple, efficient, and manageable for teachers and students alike. The systems should also serve the needs of users outside the classrooms—those who use student learning and performance information for other reasons. Our framework organizes the information teachers need to collect into three dimensions, which can be used by five different kinds of users.

Three Dimensions of Information

We believe that classroom-based, individually tailored student assessment systems need to help teachers collect three kinds of information on every student. Figure 6.1 shows these three kinds, or dimensions, of such a system. Dimension 1, skills and content, is the most traditional and familiar. Teachers need to assess what their students *know* in terms of skills and facts. Dimension 2, performance, requires teachers to assess what students can *do*—how students use those skills and facts in real situations both inside and outside school. Dimension 3, self-understanding, is a link between Dimensions 1 and 2. Teachers need to assess how students *understand* their own learning—how they learn well, what they need to help them learn well, and what they need when learning seems hard or confusing.

Five Kinds of Users

These three kinds of information are used by five kinds of stakeholders: school districts, state education agencies, and sometimes state legislatures; teachers; schools; parents; and students. The tricky part for teachers is that each stakeholder needs slightly different information about student learning. The challenge is to develop a system for each classroom or teacher team to collect information about what students know, do, and understand to meet the needs of all five user groups.

What information do these stakeholders need? Districts, state agencies, and legislatures ask for systematically generated and summarized information about all students' learning for various types of accountability. Increasingly, state departments of education, usually at the urging of legislatures, are holding schools accountable for achieving learning gain targets as measured by statewide curriculum-based tests or the familiar achievement tests. Schools that do not meet targets risk a decrease in resources or worse.

| 6.1 | Three Dimensions of an Individually Tailored, Classroom-Based Assessment System |

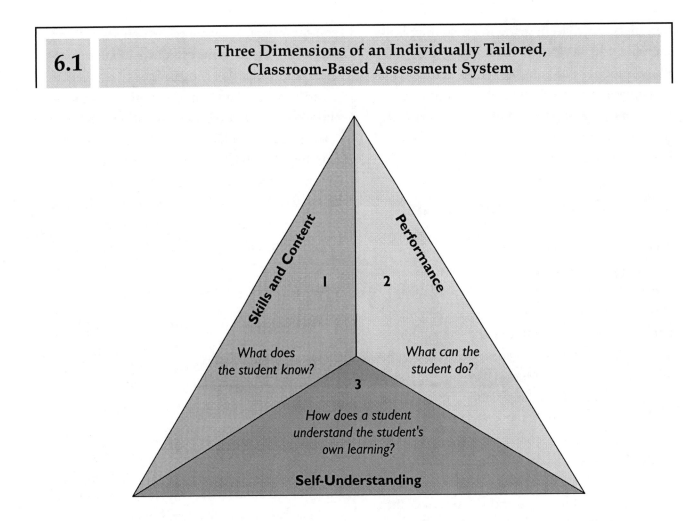

Teachers need to have information about how students learn so they can identify and collectively plan how to better support learning growth in their classrooms. At the school level, teachers may need to examine their classroom assessment practices in various areas to make sure that they can compare the information from class to class.

In one school where Ms. Jackson worked, teachers spent a year investigating and developing a common approach to assessing reading comprehension to complement the fluency measures they were already using. By working together to align their classroom-based systems, they were able to compare growth across classrooms and grades and to target areas that needed more attention and resources. The school improvement plan the next year included goals and activities to address these weak spots in their overall literacy program.

Parents like to know that their sons and daughters are learning and growing. They usually want to know how their children are learning compared to other students in the class or of a similar age. Most parents are also interested in learning whether their children enjoy school. Students need to know what they are expected to learn, how well they are accomplishing those tasks, and what strategies they need to develop to learn well. Figure 6.2 shows the five different users of information generated by a teacher's assessment system and summarizes how each group applies that information.

How Do Educators Obtain Such Information?

Teachers are experimenting with many new strategies and a few old ones for collecting information. This book cannot adequately address all the strategies that are currently in use, but we have listed some in Figure 6.3. Notice that some strategies work well in all three dimensions, while others tend to generate information for only one or two dimensions. Understanding the strategies that have multiple uses and those that don't can help teachers select the set of strategies that will be most efficient and effective for their classrooms.

We recommend that teachers discuss the strategies shown in Figure 6.3 among their colleagues. Which are familiar, and which need further exploration? Confusion sometimes arises when the same words have different meanings to different teachers, school districts, and states. Do all the teachers and staff in your school mean the same thing by "journaling," "mind maps," or "curriculum-based assessment"? If not, discussion and further exploration—perhaps beginning with some of the resources we provide here—can help. The point is to develop a common language with colleagues and to widen the options available for collecting and recording student learning and performance information. Unfortunately, teachers cannot always use the same strategies for all students.

Some approaches—among them portfolios, student conferences, and student goal setting—do work well with most students, and many of the same strategies can be used to document learning of students with disabilities. There are other inventories, tests, and diagnostic tools that classroom teachers or specialists—school psychologists, speech and language professionals, and therapists—can use to generate information for designing student learning as well. With a big enough tool kit, teachers will be able to select those strategies that best fit the classroom and individual students.

We make a distinction between assessments *for* student learning and those *of* student learning. Assessments *of* student learning give teachers information about the skills and abilities students bring with them to their learning. Such assessments help teachers design curriculum and instruction.

Assessments *for* student learning give teachers information about the learning progress students are actually making. Of course, just as curriculum and teaching decisions intertwine, assessment *of* student learning generates information for making ongoing decisions *for* student learning.

6.2   Five Users of Classroom-Based Assessment Systems

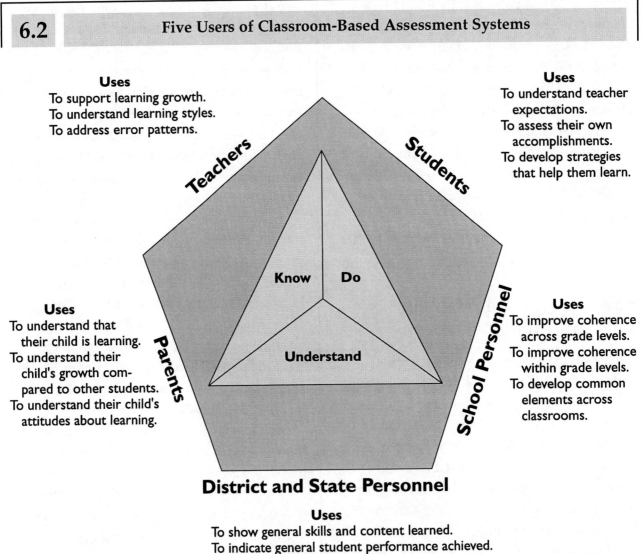

Uses
To support learning growth.
To understand learning styles.
To address error patterns.

Uses
To understand teacher
   expectations.
To assess their own
   accomplishments.
To develop strategies
   that help them learn.

Teachers

Students

Know | **Do**

Understand

Uses
To understand that
   their child is learning.
To understand their
   child's growth com-
   pared to other students.
To understand their child's
   attitudes about learning.

Parents

School Personnel

Uses
To improve coherence
   across grade levels.
To improve coherence
   within grade levels.
To develop common
   elements across
   classrooms.

District and State Personnel

Uses
To show general skills and content learned.
To indicate general student performance achieved.
To assess parents' satisfaction with student learning.

Even though some tools and strategies work for both, important differences exist. Assessment *for* student learning typically begins when teachers start collecting information on a new student.

They must figure out what the student knows and can do, how the student learns best, and what learning situations or strategies are most likely to be successful, or even unsuccessful.

6.3   Strategies for Collecting Student Information

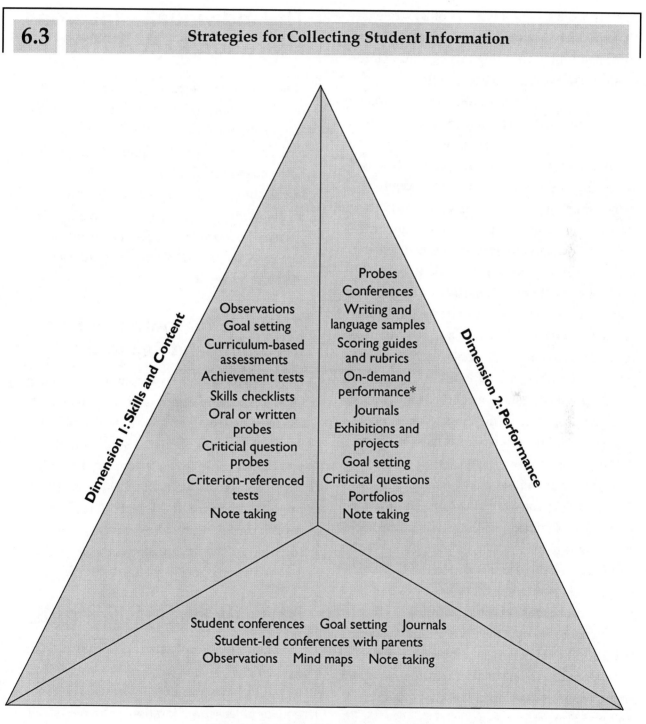

Dimension 1: Skills and Content

Dimension 2: Performance

Observations
Goal setting
Curriculum-based assessments
Achievement tests
Skills checklists
Oral or written probes
Criticial question probes
Criterion-referenced tests
Note taking

Probes
Conferences
Writing and language samples
Scoring guides and rubrics
On-demand performance*
Journals
Exhibitions and projects
Goal setting
Criticical questions
Portfolios
Note taking

Student conferences   Goal setting   Journals
Student-led conferences with parents
Observations   Mind maps   Note taking

Dimension 3: Self-Understanding

*A requested performance that is not part of a test.

The tests, diagnostic tools, and other strategies that special educators and specialists use are most helpful for acquiring this beginning information. The ABA Inventory and the History/Transition Information Profile explained in Chapter 2 are also tools to generate assessment information for student learning.

Assessment *of* student learning is the ongoing evaluation and assessment of student progress and academic achievement aligned with the curriculum and district or state standards. This continuous assessment gives teachers the information they need to make daily or weekly decisions about how to adjust their teaching or support so that students are successful. Oral and written probes, observations, and classroom tests or quizzes are among the tools teachers might use to gather this information.

Different combinations of the strategies listed in Figure 6.3, along with others teachers may already be using, will work for most students. There are also likely to be groups of students, who cluster into either mixed-ability or same-ability groups, for whom the same strategies will work. For example, if several students are second-language learners, or are struggling readers, like Jamie, Nadine, and Brandon in Ms. Clark's class, teachers might want to use extra oral or written probes for checking learning.

A classroom may have a few students who need additional documentation for some part of their learning. To help collect information about them, we have developed the Individually Tailored Education Report (ITER).

The Individually Tailored Education Report (ITER)

Students who require frequent and focused curricular decisions might be officially designated as "eligible for special education" and require an individualized education plan (IEP). The ITER helps meet official IEP requirements, while tracking teaching decisions and learning accomplishments. With the addition of a district's cover page and other minor adjustments, the ITER can also serve as the IEP because it includes the required information.

Rationale for Individualized Recording and Reporting

Only a few students require an ITER. Some may need this level of depth only when they and their teachers are trying to solve a particularly difficult learning problem, such as a student who freezes up when it comes to math, or a student who resists and rebels when involved in cooperative projects. When we developed the ITER, we had several common problems we wanted to solve: IEPs' lack of curriculum focus, disuse of IEPs, and excessive paperwork needed for IEPs.

IEPs' Lack of Curriculum Focus

Many IEPs emphasize skill acquisition that assessments *for* learning had shown needed mastery. IEPs have traditionally focused on remediation, or at least amelioration, of students' deficiencies and delays. What has been missing is a clear link between the goals and objectives of IEPs and the curriculum and standards other students in the schools pursue.

When the federal special education law, the Individuals with Disabilities Education Act (IDEA), was reauthorized by Congress in 1997, it contained a new requirement to increase the access of students with disabilities to the general education curriculum. The logic behind the new requirement is that although students with disabilities might learn differently and to different degrees of mastery than students without disabilities, they should be working toward the same curriculum standards and expectations as all other students. We believe the ITER solves this problem of disconnect from the general education curriculum by designing specific student learning objectives for students with disabilities at the same time that the curriculum and learning activities for students in the general education classroom are being developed.

The Disappearing IEP

Individualized education plans have served many important functions for students and their families. Unfortunately, schools do not always provide appropriate educational services until parents, students, and school personnel sit down together and develop an IEP, which indicates the school's commitment to provide such support and reflects parents' and students' understanding of student needs.

Despite some usefulness, however, IEPs often become more a way for schools to comply with the requirements of federal special education law and regulations than a dynamic teaching tool that supports teachers' curriculum, teaching plan, and delivery. Too many IEPs get filed away as soon as the IEP meeting is over and don't reappear until the next meeting is scheduled.

We believe the ITER solves this problem of disuse by encouraging IEP teams to write broad annual goals and a few initial learning objectives and leaving the articulation of specific learning objectives until the general education curriculum has been determined. Student learning is then tied to the general education curriculum, and learning targets are developed as general education decisions are made. This process makes the ITER version of an IEP a more dynamic document, which records student learning gains and devises new and revises old learning objectives throughout the year.

Too Much Paperwork

Perhaps the most common complaint of teachers, especially special education teachers, is *too much paperwork!* We think the ITER can lighten the paperwork load by sharing the responsibility for its writing among teachers and students. For example, Ms. Clark's team devised Susannah's learning objectives during their planning meeting, and Ms. Jackson filled them in on the ITER. Later, during the activities and lessons, Ms. Clark and some of Susannah's peers filled in what Susannah actually learned. Figure 6.4, on page 104, shows Susannah's ITER for the unit on Egypt.

As in Susannah's case, the ITER can be used throughout the instructional period or term, updating outcomes and developing new teaching objectives that are responsive to the student's changing needs and abilities. The ITER can also be used on-the-spot to help analyze and plan instruction when individual student learning issues arise. We know a teacher in a supervisory role who is using the ITER to teach and guide classroom assistants to help them pay particular attention to individual students during a given lesson.

As the figure shows, the ITER becomes a longitudinal record of class activities, Susannah's learning objectives within those activities, and ongoing progress and outcomes. Student progress also reflects incidental learning and notable interactions among classmates. Recording these unanticipated results for Susannah provided a more complete report for her parents when the team sent a copy of this ITER home at the end of the grading period.

An ITER varies in length, from one to many pages. Sometimes writing a single goal on one page and logging teaching objectives and student accomplishments as they emerge make sense. Another option is to cluster several goals on a page that relate to a curriculum theme or area, then record all the related teaching objectives as they emerge. However it's used, the ITER fulfills the requirements of the IEP, because *at any point in time, teachers have a complete set of annual goals and current teaching objectives.*

The ITER can also help fulfill the new requirement for states to have alternative assessment systems for the small number of students (usually 1–2 percent of all students) who cannot take the official state assessments required by federal special education law and regulations. Different states are approaching this requirement in different ways, and the ITER may or may not fit a state's alternative assessment plan. The reasoning for requiring alternative assessments is that teachers should be held accountable for making sure that students with disabilities learn the same curriculum and work toward the same standards as all other students.

Although many students with complicated and challenging disabilities will not learn the same amount or to the same degree of mastery as other students, they can and should work toward the same standards in ways that can enhance, enable, and enrich their lives. The ITER is one way to document such learning and could serve as part of a portfolio that some states (e.g., Kentucky) are developing for their alternative assessment systems.

The ITER Summary

A second document that can actually *save* teachers time is the ITER Summary. An example is shown in Figure 6.5, on page 106. As teachers work with the curriculum decisions discussed in this book, over time they will end up with a small stack of folders for roughly one-fifth of their students. Each time they sit down to brainstorm new teaching plans or review student accomplishments, teachers will probably grab the stack of folders to remind themselves or the planning group about the unique learning requirements of those few students who need the most careful and systematic thinking and decisions.

Teachers can use the ITER Summary in a number of ways. We originally put it on a 5" × 8" card as a handy, quick reference to show a student's annual goals. Some teachers keep the card in their grade book, so that when they plan or think about their teaching, they are reminded to reflect on how teaching decisions might affect some learners.

Figure 6.5 illustrates Susannah's ITER Summary for the 1999–2000 school year. Her general education teacher made several copies to give to other teachers who also work with Susannah, so that all can be reminded of Susannah's unique learning needs and preferences. Some of her teachers also track these objectives on Susannah's ITER, which becomes part of, or a supporting document to, Susannah's complete IEP and portfolio.

Who Fills Out the ITER?

Who fills out the ITER (and ITER Summary) for students using IEPs depends on how inclusive the school has become. In schools where special education teachers support integrating students with disabilities into general education classrooms, special education teachers might complete the annual goals part of an ITER during an IEP meeting. Teachers can then continue to use the ITER as a working document to plan and record emerging teaching objectives. In some situations, special educators write down such teaching objectives for the general education teacher, and in other situations the general education teacher may begin using the ITER and the

ITER Summary herself. A classroom assistant may have a role in completing the ITER.

In situations characterized more by integration than inclusion—where special educators are primarily responsible for determining teaching objectives—it is also likely that the IEP team will complete the summary and then pass it on to all the other teachers and staff who work with the students in the course of their day.

In schools that have more completely restructured so that teams of teachers, each with different expertise, work together with large groups of diverse students, the student's primary teacher will likely be the one who initiates the ITER. All the teachers and other staff on the team may contribute teaching objectives and record student accomplishments. In some situations, the teacher team may have requested outside consultative support from other specialists (such as therapists or experts who provide communication or behavioral supports) who will help the team design teaching objectives. The ITER and the ITER Summary become ongoing working documents used by the whole team to ensure a well-tailored curriculum and individually effective learning experiences for any student the team thinks needs a more focused and systematic approach.

Scoring *All* Students Against High Standards

Earlier in this chapter, we discussed the current standards-based reforms. The impetus for this national trend is clearly the desire to improve the learning outcomes of children and youth. But we

6.4 Example of an Individually Tailored Education Report (ITER)

Student Name: *Susannah Walsh*   Year: *1999–2000*

Present abilities: *Susannah is a fluent reader—approximately 120 wpm on a 4th grade passage. She is learning to use a Franklin Speller and to spell check her work on the computer. Susannah successfully uses social stories to help her communicate with peers. She is practicing techniques to aid in the clarity of her speech intelligibility.*

Preferences, interests, learning style, needed supports, and transition needs: *Susannah loves to work with peers. She enjoys working on a computer. Her favorite leisure activities are looking at clothes and jewelry in catalogs and magazines, singing, and cooking. She works best when she buddies-up, using visuals, lists, and a daily schedule with pictures of her activities.*

Annual goals:
1. Expand her vocabulary within the context of curriculum themes and topics.
2. Demonstrate social skills while interacting with peers and staff (e.g., initiate and maintain conversations, take turns, and make eye contact).
3. Use strategies to increase her reading and listening comprehension.

How goals relate to *Susannah's life: Susannah needs to understand and use vocabulary related to personal information and self-management. She needs to practice interacting with peers and adults for later jobs and social activities. Susannah needs support strategies for understanding basic safety and community information.*

Curricular area: *Language Arts*

Date	Class or Theme Activities	Goals Within Activities	Evaluation or Assessment Methods	Progress and Accomplishment Within Activities
1/12/00	*Read background information on Egypt and use vocabulary and spelling within the unit.*	*Susannah will work with a partner to read information and answer "who," "what," "when," and "where" questions, using a highlighter.*	*Photocopied reading pages with target information highlighted.*	*1/15/00: Susannah read Chapter 1 with a peer helper (Anna). She highlighted target information with peer prompting about half the time.*
		Susannah will recognize and explain five new vocabulary words per chapter.	*Make an oral presentation. Match definitions to words. Use words in oral or written sentences.*	*1/18/00: Susannah picked out the five vocabulary words in her reading, using a list of target words to look for. She explained three of five target words orally. She matched three of five words to their definitions.*

6.4 Example of an Individually Tailored Education Report (ITER)—continued

Date	Class or Theme Activities	Goals Within Activities	Evaluation or Assessment Methods	Progress and Accomplishment Within Activities
1/20/00	Use the computer program Inspiration to make a web of information on Egypt.	Susannah will use the list of "who," "what," "when," and "where" questions to help organize a web of Egypt.	A completed web.	1/24/00: Susannah accurately placed information in her web when a peer assisted her with color-coded list text boxes.
		Susannah will ask the peer assistant and teacher for help if she needs it.	Teacher observation.	Susannah asked for help at least 75 percent of the time she needed it. She needed instructions broken into simple steps, which the teacher had to initiate.
1/27/00	Queen Hattie project	Susannah will work in a small group to read a chapter, create a list of at least five pieces of regalia, and choose pictures to cut and paste for a poster.	Queen Hattie scoring guide (negotiated with the teacher).	2/8/00: Susannah used a picture-symbol guide to identify items in the text. She chose several pictures to cut and paste for her poster. She scored a "4" on her scoring guide!! (She loved it.)
		Susannah will communicate with peers, initiating and maintaining topics appropriate to the activity and group.	Teacher observation.	Some personality conflicts caused problems in her group of three. Susannah required a social story to help her recognize using "words that hurt." She initiated conversation at least four times each 40-minute session. She responded to about 50 percent of peer-initiated conversations.
2/12/00	Prepare a Middle-Eastern feast.	Susannah will follow directions to prepare a recipe.	Completed preparation of food and teacher observation.	2/12/00: Susannah followed a recipe. She broke it down into single steps and put it into a list format.
		Susannah will make herself understood to visitors she doesn't know by using her techniques of slow and exaggerated speech.	Visitor report and observations by a speech-language professional.	Susannah needed prompting by a speech-language professional to slow and exaggerate her speech. The visitor understood Susannah in two of five instances.
2/15/00	Belly dancing.	Susannah will interact socially with peers in a large-group setting.	Teacher observation.	2/15/00: Susannah did a great job initiating, responding, and taking her turn during a 40-minute activity. What fun!

6.5	Example of an ITER Summary

Individually Tailored Education Report (ITER) Summary

Student Name: *Susannah Walsh*   Year: *1999-2000*

Present abilities: *Susannah is a fluent reader—about 120 wpm on 4th grade material. She can make her speech understood when she slows her rate of speech and over-articulates or exaggerates her speech. She can use a word processing program with spell check and is learning to use a Franklin Speller. She can produce simple sentences orally and written sentences when prompted.*

Preferences, interests, learning styles, needed supports, and transition needs: *Susannah is very visual. She works well with lists and schedules with paired picture & word. Highlighters work well when looking for key information in reading. Social stories help with social communication (see her social stories binder and school-day picture schedule). Susannah loves to work with peers. She likes fashion, singing, and cooking.*

Goals	Reasons for Focusing on These Goals and Their Connections to Life
1. *Communicate and interact socially.*	*Susannah has problems with peer relationships. She would like some friends to hang out with.*
2. *Articulate clearly.*	*Susannah gets frustrated when people don't understand her speech. It created problems in her cafeteria job.*
3. *Comprehend written and spoken information.*	*Susannah has trouble picking out relevant information when listening and reading. She needs to work on these areas for safety and self-management.*
4. *Learn computer skills.* 5. 6. 7.	*Susannah has difficulty with the motor act of writing and with organizing information. Specific software can support these needs.*

are concerned about the implications for those students who might never meet—or in some cases come close to—some of those standards.

Despite requirements in the Individuals with Disabilities Education Act (IDEA) to provide accommodations and modifications that help students with disabilities demonstrate what they know and can do, there is a temptation for districts to excuse these students from meeting the benchmarks, standards, and other traditional hallmarks of achievement and success. Simply put, setting higher achievement standards increases the risk that more students will not meet them, and will subsequently endure the concomitant stigmas of failure. The challenge becomes how to encourage achievement and engender success, rather than punishing inability for some learners who will not meet stated standards in the required ways.

One Solution: A Generic Scoring Guide

We hope that high standards become goals, not barriers or burdens, for students. We also hope that educational reforms encourage teachers to constantly support children on the frontiers of their personal learning adventures, and identify what students do learn that might not have been predicted. To this end, we offer a generic scoring guide (Figure 6.6) as a basis for rethinking how to describe, document, and characterize student efforts.

Many of the scoring guides we see teachers using are thinly disguised grading systems:

Instead of an *A* or an *F,* a student now gets a "6" or a "1," with performance descriptions that focus on how the product or performance falls short of the mark. Furthermore, these scoring guides have not eliminated a teacher's dilemma of how to score the student who far exceeded anyone's expectations on a given task—yet did not meet benchmarks—or the capable student who did not complete the assignment.

Used with task descriptions designed for specific student products or presentations, the generic scoring guide provides several types of flexibility:

• All students are focused on a benchmark set for acceptable performance (a score of "5").

• Students can negotiate areas within a specific task to focus their individual work and practice on.

• The scoring guide allows students with disabilities, who might never meet the benchmark, to still consistently obtain scores above the middle (a score of "4"), encouraging positive feelings and learning.

Judgments such as "exceeds expectations," "exemplary work," or "discrepant with previous accomplishments" are validated with narrative descriptions from one or more reviewers, providing more complete information about the meaning of the score. The scoring guide avoids pejorative descriptors to characterize student efforts and accomplishments (e.g., "superficial," "severely limited," or "rarely if ever"). Students with disabilities can score as high as or higher than nonlabeled students on any given product

6.6	A Generic Scoring Guide to Encourage Achievement

Score	Performance Assessment Description
6	Strong and exemplary work. *(Wow! You've really outdone yourself!)* Exceeded expectations in all or most components of the project requirements. Contributed a "unique signature" to the final product or performance.
5	Proficient. *(You got it!)* Met benchmarks in all areas covered by the product or presentation.
4	Developing capacity. *(You're almost there.)* Work reflected efforts and accomplishments in all standard components of the product or performance, but one or more areas did not meet benchmarks.
3	Developing more. *(You're getting closer.)* Worked on and completed specifically negotiated components of the product or performance. Results reflected substantial personal improvement and learning gains.
2	Developing. *(Keep going.)* Worked on and completed specifically negotiated components of the product or performance to a satisfactory degree. Met expectations.
1	Exploring. *(You may need some help.)* Participated, but the final product or performance reflected significant discrepancies with previous accomplishments.
0	Did not submit a performance or product.

Note: A score of "0," "1," "2," "3," or "6" requires documentation to justify the score, including a description of specific negotiated components and accomplishments and an explanation of how expectations were either exceeded or not met.

or presentation—using negotiated expectations—without compromising benchmarked performance standards.

Used across a term or year on a range of projects, a student's cumulative scores provide a sense of a student's overall accomplishments in relation to accepted standards and benchmarks. Even students with disabilities or other learning challenges, who may never achieve the standard the way most students will, can end the year with a record of growth and accomplishment toward the standards without experiencing the kind of failure and discouragement that usually accompanies the grading and scoring of less-accomplished performance.

Ms. Clark takes these considerations into account in the scoring guide she used with the Queen Hattie project for her unit on Egypt (Figure 6.7).

Using the Scoring Guide

Ms. Clark explains, "We developed our scoring guide for the Queen Hattie project in a 10-minute brainstorming session as a whole class. We generally do this work when I first present an activity. The class is familiar with the generic scoring guide. By creating their own guide, the students are better able to understand the task and assessment expectations. Our general guidelines for a scoring guide range from *Wow! You've really outdone yourself!* (an exemplary '6'), to *You're almost there* (a developing '4'), to *You may need some help* (an exploring or minimal '1').

"I might also choose to use the Queen Hattie project as a work sample to demonstrate learning for the state benchmark in reading comprehension. Figure 6.8, on page 112, shows our state's scoring guide for this benchmark. The two scoring guides are slightly different. The state guide uses a score of '4' for 'proficient' and has two levels above proficient. Although this is a typical scoring guide, it does not provide for less able learners to score in the middle. In fact, some of our students would rarely get more than a '1' or '2.'

"Within my classroom, and for many projects, I can use the logic of the generic scoring guide. If I decide to use a project as a work sam-

ple, I can switch to the state scoring guide. By using this authentic piece of learning (the Queen Hattie project), I can satisfy my need to know how much and what kind of learning have taken place and also satisfy the state's desire to confirm that my students are making individual progress and are learning within the range of their peers. I can also use the generic scoring guide and translate the student's work to the state scoring guide at a different time. It's easy to translate my 6-point scale to the state's 6-point scale for those students who meet or exceed the benchmark. For those who are not yet that successful, I can support their ongoing enthusiasm and motivation by using our scoring guide, which rewards them with scores of '3' and '4' even though they haven't yet accomplished the benchmark."

Ms. Clark Ends the Year

Finally, the last day of the school year is drawing near. Ms. Clark and her team of specialists and support personnel share a late lunch on an early-release planning day in May. They begin talking about how to bring closure to the year. This time, Ms. Andrews, a 7th grade language arts block teacher, joins the group. Ms. Andrews will be teaching many of Ms. Clark's students next year.

Ms. Clark suggests that the group tell Ms. Andrews about the class, at least in general terms. She also asks that they save some time to tell Ms. Andrews a few specifics about the more challenging students.

Ms. Clark and the teaching team filled out a History/Transition Information Profile (explained

| | 6.7 | Ms. Clark's Scoring Guide for the Queen Hattie Project |

Score	Performance Assessment Description
6	*Strong and Exemplary Work.* I understood the description of Queen Hattie. My list included at least 40 details of her coronation outfit. My picture is accurate and shows care and commitment to the project. I included additional detail to make my picture above the standard. My work is strong. *I nailed it!*
5	*Proficient.* I met the standard. My list included at least 30 details from the story. My picture is good and included a few background details that show other information about the time. My work is proficient. *I got it!*
4	*Developing Capacity.* I understood the description of Queen Hattie. My list included at least 25 details from the story. My picture looks like Hattie and is fairly detailed. *I am getting it!*
3	*Developing More.* I pretty much understood the description of Queen Hattie. My list included at least 20 details. I drew a pretty good picture of Hattie. I may have left out a couple of things, but I got the basic project done. My work has some strong parts. *I made an attempt!*
2	*Developing.* I think I understood the description of Queen Hattie. My list included at least 15 details. My picture was okay but could have been more detailed. *I met expectations.*
1	*Exploring.* I didn't get very involved in this project. I didn't understand the description of Queen Hattie. My list was incomplete. *I did not meet expectations.*
0	Did not submit a performance or product.

in Chapter 2) for Susannah and three of her classmates for whom Ms. Clark thought the additional information would be helpful. Ms. Andrews received these records and had a chance to skim them. She also received the activity-based assessments completed earlier in the year, and her quick skim is helping her get a feel for the stu-

dents and their families. Ms. Hendricks, the special education teacher at the middle school, and Ms. Jackson will continue to work with the group as they move on to grade 7.

The conversation gets lively. Ms. Jackson and Ms. Hendricks take turns describing the students and offering anecdotal information about individual kids. Ms. Jackson shares a beautifully drawn mind map that Brandon recently created as a literature response during her reading group. She explains, "When given the opportunity to use his considerable artistic talent, Brandon is capable of producing exceptional work."

Ms. Clark reminisces about the beginning of the year and her many failures and successes with Susannah: "I'm happy to pass along a record [Susannah's ITER] of what worked and what didn't." She then begins to relate a recent story about Brandon that captures the whole year for the group. There have been some remarkably rewarding times for everyone, including Brandon.

One of the group's concerns is the approach of the state assessment tests in writing. Ms. Clark reminds the group how they all struggle every year with the inequities they find in the test.

She asks, "How do we score students with various educational plans? Several of my students have wonderful, bright minds and good ideas, but to get an idea written on paper is sometimes an unrealistic expectation. I have the option of modifying writing tests and then marking those tests separately for official state recording. I explained to all my students the requirements of the test and told them I would like them to do the very best they could, and then we could decide if they wanted some help or not. I talked to them about the importance of all the writing components, especially voice. No one wants to read words without a voice.

"Everyone was primed to take the test. Desks were separated, pencils sharpened, and extra paper placed on desks. Ms. Jackson worked with me to read the topic choices to several students. While several students whined that they didn't like the topics, Brandon perked up. He decided to write about the time that he set a goal for himself. Amazingly, this usual nonwriter sat for 30 minutes and laboriously wrote a page and a half about the time he wanted to buy a motorcycle. His dad had agreed to match whatever he could earn. He wrote about how he went around the neighborhood with a lawnmower and how nobody was interested in paying him to mow the lawn.

"Brandon never asked for help until he had finished. He raised his hand and asked if I would correct it for him. As I started to read my way through the painfully formed letters, I was nearly overwhelmed with excitement. I could actually read this paper! The idea was clear, the organization was strong, and the voice was powerful. It would be difficult, but I believed that a scorer could figure it out. Brandon looked imploringly at me and said, 'Will you fix any words they won't know?'

"I explained that if I did that, I would have to mark his test differently from the others. 'I can read this, Brandon!'

"He countered, 'Can you fix *lawnmower*? I want them to know it's a lawnmower.'

"On the state's official scoring guide, Brandon's narrative scored '4's in voice, ideas, and content, and '3's across the board in all other areas except for conventions, which received one lone '2.' The best part of the test for Brandon and his parents was the missing 'M' on the essay, which I did not have to mark to indicate 'modification needed.'"

	6.8	A Typical State Reading or Literature Scoring Guide

Score	Description of Response
6	**The response demonstrates a thorough understanding of the parts of the selection and the selection as a whole.** *The response:* Indicates a thorough and accurate understanding of main ideas and all significant supporting details, including clarification of complexities. Draws subtle as well as obvious inferences and forms insightful conclusions about their meaning. Presents interpretations, generalizations, or predictions based on specific and compelling evidence. Uses relevant and specific information from textual resources (e.g., table of contents, graphs, charts, diagrams, glossary) to form interpretations and deepen understanding.
5	**The response demonstrates a strong understanding of the parts of the selection and the selection as a whole.** *The response:* Indicates a thorough and accurate understanding of main ideas and significant supporting details. Draws key inferences and forms strongly supported conclusions about their meaning. Presents interpretations, generalizations, or predictions based on specific, conclusive evidence. Uses information from textual resources (e.g., table of contents, graphs, charts, diagrams, glossary) to form interpretations and deepen understanding.
4	**The response demonstrates a competent and proficient understanding of the parts of the selection and the selection as a whole.** *The response:* Indicates an understanding of the main ideas and relevant and specific supporting details. Draws obvious inferences and forms supported conclusions about their meaning. Presents interpretations, generalizations, or predictions based on adequate evidence. Uses information from textual resources (e.g., table of contents, graphs, charts, diagrams, glossary) to clarify meaning and form conclusions.

| 6.8 | A Typical State Reading or Literature Scoring Guide—*continued* |

Score	Description of Response
3	**The response demonstrates a limited, inconsistent, or incomplete understanding of the parts of the selection and the selection as a whole.** *The response:* Correctly identifies some main ideas; focuses on isolated details or misunderstands or omits some significant supporting details. Suggests inferences but provides incomplete support for conclusions based on them. Suggests interpretations, generalizations, or predictions, but provides incomplete support for them. Uses obvious information from textual resources (e.g., table of contents, graphs, charts, diagrams, glossary) to gain meaning, but may overlook some important details.
2	**The response demonstrates a confused or inaccurate understanding of the parts of the selection and the selection as a whole.** *The response:* Shows a confused, inaccurate, or fragmented understanding of the selection; presents random, incomplete, or irrelevant evidence. Does not draw inferences or suggests inferences not supported by the text. Does not provide supported interpretations, generalizations, or predictions, or provides ones that are unsupported by the text; may contain passages copied verbatim without analysis or commentary. Does not refer to textual resources (e.g., table of contents, graphs, charts, diagrams, glossary), or reveals that the reader is distracted or confused by them.
I	**The response demonstrates virtually no understanding of the parts of the selection and the selection as a whole.** *The response:* Does not show an ability to construct a literal meaning of the selection; may focus only on reader's own frustration or indicate that the reader gave up.

Source: Oregon Department of Education.

A reflective silence fell over the group. Brandon's success on the writing test had been hard won, but it was wonderful. Everyone had worked hard, and in the end, the entire class had done well on all the tests. It was a satisfying way to end the year.

Ms. Clark broke the silence: "What's everyone doing this summer? Will there be time for a little vacation after summer school?"

As the group began to break up, everyone seemed to be talking at once: "the lake for a few days," "reorganize my files," "a workshop on _____," "a little time in my garden." Fall seemed refreshingly far away.

* * *

Today's schools are pressured to focus on improving student learning. We applaud this new attention to results. At the same time, as we have pointed out in this chapter, doing so for every child is complex and full of risks. We hope the ideas offered in this book provide teachers with useful tactics for working through these complexities and risks in ways that help students learn and feel accomplished and that minimize students' experience of failure and inadequacy.

For Further Reading

Part 1: Assessment

The book by Wiggins and McTighe (1998) and the accompanying handbook by McTighe and Wiggins (1999) examine what understanding is and how it differs from knowing. The authors discuss how teachers can know that students truly understand and can apply their knowledge in meaningful ways. The book provides the conceptual foundation, and the handbook offers the practical side, with a planning template, worksheets, and exercises.

The following books and articles by Wiggins describe topics within assessment: Wiggins (1998), learner-centered assessments; Wiggins (1997), work-design standards; Wiggins (1996a), exemplars; and Wiggins (1996b), accountability.

Four books discuss policies and practices related to the inclusion of students with disabilities in large-scale assessment programs, alternative assessment, and authentic assessment: Darling-Hammond, Ancess, and Falk (1995); Goodwin (1997); Landau, Voss, and Romano (1998); and Legin and Shoemaker (1999).

The article by McLaughlin, No let, Him, and Henderson (1999) gives a clear and concise overview of the 1997 Individual with Disabilities Education Act provisions. The resource by McDonnell and McLaughlin (1997) assesses the extent to which the goals of common standards and individualized education can be reconciled.

Darling-Hammond, L., Ancess, J., & Falk, B. (1995). *Authentic assessment in action: Studies of schools and students at work.* New York: Teachers College Press.

Goodwin, A. L. (1997). *Assessment for equity and inclusion: Embracing all our children.* New York: Routledge.

Landau, J. K., Voss, J. R., & Romano, C. A. (1998). *All kids count: Including students with disabilities in statewide assessment programs.* Boston: Federation for Children with Special Needs.

Legin, L., & Shoemaker, B. J. (1999). *Great performances:*

Creating classroom-based assessment tasks. Alexandria, VA: Association for Supervision and Curriculum Development.

McDonnell, L. M., & McLaughlin, M. J. (Eds.). (1997). *Educating one and all: Students with disabilities and standards-based reform.* National Research Council. Washington, DC: National Academy Press.

McLaughlin, M. J., No let, V., Him, L. M., & Henderson, K. (1999). Integrating standards: Including all students. *Exceptional Children, 31*(3), 66–71.

McTighe, J., & Wiggins, G. (1999). *The Understanding by Design handbook.* Alexandria, VA: Association for Supervision and Curriculum Development.

Wiggins, G. (1996a). Anchoring assessment with exemplars: Why students and teachers need models. *Gifted Child Quarterly, 40*(2), 66–69.

Wiggins, G.(1996b). Embracing accountability. *New Schools, New Communities, 12*(2), 4–10.

Wiggins, G. (1997). Work standards: Why we need standards for instructional and assessment design. *NASSP Bulletin, 81*(590), 56–64.

Wiggins, G. (1998). *Educative assessment: Designing assessments to inform and improve student performance.* San Francisco: Jossey-Bass.

Wiggins, G., & McTighe, J. (1998). *Understanding by Design.* Alexandria, VA: Association for Supervision and Curriculum Development.

Part 2: Teacher Inquiry

Schools and professionals that engage in inquiry examine their practices daily to identify goals and steps they must take to bring about improvement. This examination must be done collectively. The readings that follow provide insight into this process.

Ayers, W. C., & Miller, J. L. (1998). *A light in dark times: Maxine Greene and the unfinished conversation.* New York: Teachers College Press.

Duckworth, E. (1999). Engaging learners with their own ideas: An interview with Eleanor Duckworth. *Active Learner: A Foxfire Journal for Teachers, 4*(1), 28–30.

Duckworth, E., & The Experienced Teachers Group. (1997*). Teacher to teacher: Learning from each other.* New York: Teachers College Press.

Ladson-Billings, G. (1994). *The Dreamkeepers.* San Francisco: Jossey-Bass.

Leiberman, A., & Miller, L. (1999). *Teachers transforming their world and their work.* New York: Teachers College Press.

Palmer, P. J. (1998). *The courage to teach: Exploring the inner landscape of a teacher's life.* San Francisco: Jossey-Bass.

Wasley, P. A. (1994). *Stirring the chalkdust: Tales of teachers changing classroom practice.* New York: Teachers College Press.

Wasley, P. A. (1999). Teaching worth celebrating. *Educational Leadership, 56*(8), 8–13.

Recommended Web Site

Figuring out what students know and can do is one of the most challenging tasks educators face, particularly when students are not able to demonstrate their learning and accomplishments in traditional ways. Despite the complexity and controversy surrounding this important aspect of education, educators are becoming more aware of the issues and more successful at addressing the challenges. The following Web site may be helpful:

http://www.coled.umn.edu/nceo/The National Center on Educational Outcomes (NCEO) was established in 1990 to provide national leadership in the identification of outcomes, indicators, and assessments to monitor educational results for all students, including students with disabilities. Since its establishment, NCEO has been

• Working with states and federal agencies to identify important outcomes of education for students with disabilities.

• Examining the participation and use of accommodations by students with disabilities in national and state assessments.

• Evaluating national and state practices in reporting assessment information on students with disabilities.

• Bridging general and special education systems as they work to increase accountability for results of education for all students.

APPENDIX

Activity-Based Assessment Inventory for Ages 9–12

Teachers: Ask students these questions for each activity: How do you do this? When? Where? Is this something you want to change? Feel free to check, circle, or underline. Make notes everywhere!

AGES 9–12
CARING FOR SELF, FRIENDS, AND FAMILY

Student Name:

Date:

BEING A FRIEND

☞ 1. INITIATING AND MAINTAINING RELATIONSHIPS

- ➤ Meeting and making friends
- ➤ Helping friends with projects or chores
- ➤ Helping friends learn new things
- ➤ Helping friends solve problems
- ➤ Having a pen pal
- ➤ Including a variety of friends in activities

☞ 2. COMMUNICATING WITH FRIENDS

- ➤ Phoning friends
- ➤ Writing letters
- ➤ Sending friends e-mail messages

☞ 3. SOCIAL ACTIVITIES

- ➤ Having or going to parties
- ➤ Spending time with friends
- ➤ Participating in team or group activities
- ➤ Having or going to sleepovers

FAMILY MEMBERSHIP

☞ 4. FAMILY FUN

- ➤ Participating in celebrations
- ➤ Visiting relatives
- ➤ Participating in vacations and holidays

☞ 5. KITCHEN

- ➤ Helping cook
- ➤ Washing or drying dishes
- ➤ Using a dishwasher
- ➤ Putting dishes away
- ➤ Helping with grocery shopping
- ➤ Putting groceries away
- ➤ Sorting recyclables
- ➤ Taking out the trash

☞ 6. BEDROOM

- ➤ Making your bed
- ➤ Picking up and putting away belongings
- ➤ Cleaning your room

☞ 7. OUTSIDE

- ➤ Doing yard work
- ➤ Bringing in firewood
- ➤ Washing the car
- ➤ Caring for your bike

☞ 8. MISCELLANEOUS

- ➤ Taking care of siblings
- ➤ Taking care of a pet
- ➤ Getting the mail
- ➤ Running errands
- ➤ Helping with laundry
- ➤ Dusting, sweeping, and vacuuming
- ➤ Helping with household projects, such as painting and washing windows

Which ones do you want to begin doing or do more?

Which ones do you want to begin doing or do more?

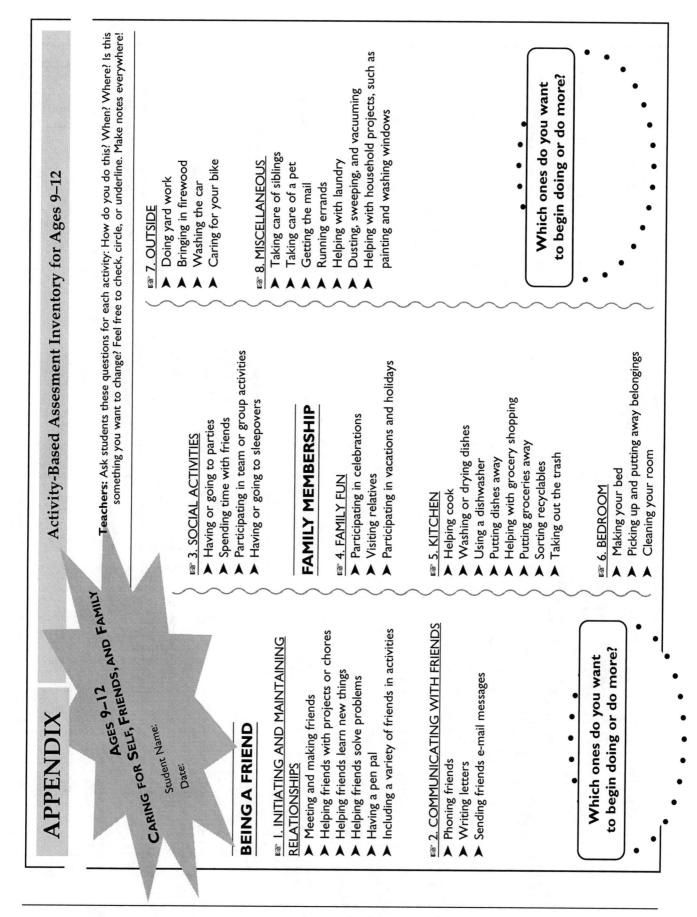

117

Activity-Based Assesment Inventory for Ages 9–12—*continued*

Teachers: Ask students these questions for each activity: How do you do this? When? Where? Is this something you want to change? Feel free to check, circle, or underline. Make notes everywhere!

AGES 9–12
AGES FOR SELF, FRIENDS, AND FAMILY
(continued)

Student Name:

Date:

PERSONAL CARE

☞ 9. MORNING AND BEDTIME
➤ Using an alarm clock
➤ Dressing and undressing
➤ Choosing clothes
➤ Taking medicine

☞ 10. BATHROOM AND GROOMING
➤ Washing face and hands
➤ Brushing teeth and flossing
➤ Blowing nose
➤ Taking baths or showers
➤ Washing and drying hair
➤ Applying deodorant
➤ Using good menstrual hygiene
➤ Using toilets in private and public bathrooms

☞ 11. PERSONAL STUFF
➤ Wearing glasses or contacts
➤ Using hearing aids
➤ Using braces
➤ Using a wheelchair
➤ Using communication devices

☞ 12. PERSONAL SAFETY
➤ Being home alone safely
➤ Following survival signs
➤ Responding to emergencies

PERSONAL MANAGEMENT

☞ 13. SCHEDULES AND APPOINTMENTS
➤ Keeping or following a calendar, schedule, or routine
➤ Going to the dentist, doctor, or nurse
➤ Getting a haircut
➤ Remembering birthdays
➤ Sending greetings to friends and family
➤ Setting personal goals and meeting them

☞ 14. ACCESSING AND USING RESOURCES
➤ Using a public library
➤ Using public transportation
➤ Finding and using "people" resources
➤ Accessing and using online computer resources
➤ Using a map
➤ Investigating and developing new leisure activities

☞ 15. MONEY
➤ Budgeting an allowance and savings
➤ Managing a bank account

☞ 16. MEALTIME
➤ Using utensils, a napkin, cup, glass, and straw
➤ Planning or ordering from a menu
➤ Paying for a meal
➤ Making own snacks or packing lunches

17. LEISURE
➤ Developing or planning activities
➤ Developing hobbies

Which ones do you want to begin doing or do more?

Which ones do you want to begin doing or do more?

Activity-Based Assessment Inventory for Ages 9–12—continued

Teachers: Ask students these questions for each activity: How do you do this? When? Where? Is this something you want to change? Feel free to check, circle, or underline. Make notes everywhere!

AGES 9–12
CONTRIBUTING TO COMMUNITY

Student Name:
Date:

SCHOOL MEMBERSHIP AND COMMITMENTS

☞ 1. SCHOOL
➤ Following arrival and departure routines
➤ Getting to and from school
➤ Following cafeteria and snack bar routines (e.g., waiting in line, choosing and carrying items, paying for meals, selecting seats, and recycling trash)
➤ Delivering school-home communications
➤ Doing homework
➤ Responding to emergency drills

☞ 2. SCHOOL JOBS AND CHORES
➤ Getting and passing out supplies
➤ Putting chairs up and down
➤ Caring for classroom pets
➤ Watering plants
➤ Erasing chalkboards
➤ Running classroom errands

> **Which ones do you want to begin doing or do more?**

➤ Helping in the cafeteria, library, office, or P.E. department
➤ Being on the litter patrol
➤ Being a custodial assistant
➤ Helping with school recycling
➤ Being a hall or room monitor
➤ Working in the school store
➤ Working on the school newspaper

☞ 3. SCHOOL PARTICIPATION
➤ Participating in or chairing a committee or club
➤ Participating in or organizing a school event or meeting

COMMUNITY MEMBERSHIP AND COMMITMENTS

☞ 4. GROUP MEMBERSHIP
➤ Attending scout or 4H club meetings
➤ Attending church or temple services and events

☞ 5. VOLUNTEERING
➤ For neighborhood beautification projects
➤ For park or beach cleanups
➤ For canned food or clothing drives
➤ To visit nursing homes, hospitals, or schools
➤ To help with church events
➤ To work in the public library

JOBS AND CAREER

☞ 6. AFTER SCHOOL AND VACATION JOBS
➤ Paper route
➤ Baby-sitting
➤ Caring for a neighbor's pet
➤ Doing yard work, shoveling snow, or stacking firewood
➤ Working in the family business
➤ Picking fruits and vegetables

> **Which ones do you want to begin doing or do more?**

APPENDIX

Activity-Based Assesment Inventory for Ages 9–12—*continued*

AGES 9–12
ENJOYING LEISURE AND RECREATION

Student Name: _____

Date: _____

Teachers: Ask students these questions for each activity: How do you do this? When? Where? Is this something you want to change? Feel free to check, circle, or underline. Make notes everywhere!

MEDIA

☞ **1. READING**
- ▲ Books
- ▲ Newspapers
- ▲ Magazines

☞ **2. LISTENING AND SPEAKING**
- ▲ Using a cassette or CD player
- ▲ Listening to stories
- ▲ Listening to books on tape
- ▲ Listening to the radio
- ▲ Using a telephone, answering machine, or pager

☞ **3. WATCHING AND INTERACTING**
- ▲ Using a TV or VCR
- ▲ Using a movie or slide projector
- ▲ Using a computer
- ▲ Using software, the Internet, CD-ROM, or e-mail

EXERCISE AND FITNESS

☞ **4. OUTDOOR RECREATION**
- ▲ Climbing trees
- ▲ Using parks and playgrounds
- ▲ Riding a bike or scooter
- ▲ Jogging
- ▲ Golfing or miniature golf
- ▲ Skating
- ▲ Swimming or diving
- ▲ Hiking or climbing
- ▲ Camping
- ▲ Fishing or hunting
- ▲ Boating or rafting
- ▲ Skiing
- ▲ Horseback riding
- ▲ Playing Frisbee or catch

☞ **5. INDOOR RECREATION**
- ▲ Aerobics
- ▲ Dance
- ▲ Yoga
- ▲ Weight lifting
- ▲ Martial arts
- ▲ Using exercise equipment or machines
- ▲ Jumping rope
- ▲ Wrestling
- ▲ Bowling

☞ **6. TEAM OR GROUP GAMES AND SPORTS**
- ▲ Track and field
- ▲ Ball games (e.g., basketball, baseball, volleyball, and football)
- ▲ Racquet games (e.g., tennis, Ping-Pong, and badminton)

Which ones do you want to begin doing or do more?

Which ones do you want to begin doing or do more?

120

Activity-Based Assessment Inventory for Ages 9-12—*continued*

AGES 9–12
LEISURE AND RECREATION
(continued)

ENJOYING LEISURE AND RECREATION
(continued)

Student Name:

Date:

Teachers: Ask students these questions for each activity: How do you do this? When? Where? Is this something you want to change? Feel free to check, circle, or underline. Make notes everywhere!

EVENTS

☞ 7. COMMUNITY
▲ Attending or participating in fairs
▲ Attending festivals, exhibits, and museums
▲ Attending and participating in community events for kids and families

☞ 8. ENTERTAINMENT
▲ Attending movies
▲ Attending events such as car rallies, pet shows, races, and air shows
▲ Visiting the zoo, planetarium, and aquarium

☞ 9. CULTURAL
▲ Attending art shows and museums
▲ Attending or participating in cultural performances such as concerts, plays, and dances

Which ones do you want to begin doing or do more?

☞ 10. SPORTS
▲ Attending or participating in sports events

☞ 11. TRAVEL
▲ Summer camps

GAMES, CRAFTS, AND HOBBIES

☞ 12. PLAYING GAMES
▲ Board games
▲ Video and computer games
▲ Toys (e.g., Lego's or dolls)

☞ 13. CREATING ART
▲ Drawing and painting
▲ Calligraphy
▲ Ceramics
▲ Woodwork or metalwork
▲ Jewelry making
▲ Stained glass
▲ Origami

☞ 14. CREATING NEEDLECRAFTS
▲ Sewing
▲ Knitting
▲ Weaving
▲ Crocheting
▲ Leatherwork

☞ 15. COLLECTING
▲ Coins
▲ Stamps
▲ Stickers
▲ Rocks
▲ Trading cards

☞ 16. PHOTOGRAPHY
▲ Using a camera
▲ Putting photos in an album

☞ 17. CONSTRUCTING OR PLAYING WITH
▲ Models
▲ Kites
▲ Puzzles

☞ 18. MUSIC
▲ Singing
▲ Playing an instrument

☞ 19. SCIENCE

☞ 20. LANGUAGES

Which ones do you want to begin doing or do more?

Index

About the Authors

Dianne Ferguson (lead author) is a professor in special education at the University of Oregon. She is also director of Academic Support and Student Services in the College of Education. She is experienced at preparing teachers, designing systems that support ongoing school improvement efforts, and managing grants, which requires coordination between universities and public schools. Ferguson has taught classes and provided consultation for general and special educators in Canada, Iceland, India, Denmark, New Zealand, and Finland. Her areas of interest and expertise include issues and strategies for school inclusion for students with disabilities, administrator and teacher support for professional development, and collaboration. Ferguson is an experienced researcher and has published research reports to investigate curriculum decision making, school improvement efforts, general education experiences of students with disabilities, and the experiences of families of students with disabilities. Ferguson can be reached at College of Education, 1215 University of Oregon, Eugene, OR 97403-1215; phone: 541-346-2491; fax: 541-346-2471; e-mail: diannef@oregon.uoregon.edu.

Cleo Droege has been a middle school language arts block teacher for eight years. After teaching for three years, she left public education to work with Dianne Ferguson at the University of Oregon, where she rounded out the research team as the "regular ed" person. During her four years at Oregon, she drew on the best of both worlds of education. Four years ago, Droege returned to teaching middle school. Now her classes are larger and include more needy students. She continues using the teaching practices she developed at the University of Oregon to teach her diverse population of students. Droege can be reached at Lincoln Middle School, 1565 South 4th Street, Cottage Grove, OR 97424-2999; phone: 541-942-3316; fax: 541-9801; e-mail: cdroege@lane.k12.or.us.

Hafdís Guðjónsdóttir is assistant professor of Education and director of the Division of Developmental Education at the Iceland University of Education (IUE). She worked for 20 years as a general classroom teacher and special educator in elementary and high schools. Her focus is on inclusion, curriculum development, differentiated learning, teaching mixed-ability classes, cooperative learning, authentic assessment, mathematics for all students, teacher professionalism, school change, and collaboration with families. She currently consults on inclusion with educators in Latvia and on preparing distance education courses and teacher exchange with Norwegian educators. Current research and writing projects include mathematics for all learners and self-study of framing professional discourse with teachers. She has presented her work at local, regional, and international conferences. Guðjónsdóttir can be reached at Iceland University of Education, Stakkahlid, 105 Reykjavik, Iceland; phone: 011-354-563-3800; fax: 011-354-563-3833; e-mail: hafdisg@khi.is.

Jackie Lester has had many roles in special and general education over the past 16 years in Oregon's public schools. She has worked with

preschool through graduate-level students and has collaborated with the University of Oregon's Schools Projects. Lester is leaving her position as a speech-language pathologist and reading specialist to become the principal of a preschool through 8th grade rural school. She has worked extensively in the areas of language and literacy, attempting to bridge the gap between special education services and language support needed within general education classrooms. Lester can be reached at Dorena Elementary School, 37141 Row River Road, Cottage Grove, OR 97434-9801; phone: 541-946-1506; fax: 541-946-1507; e-mail: jlester@lane.k12.or.us.

Gwen Meyer is a senior research assistant in special education at the University of Oregon. She has 30 years of experience working with persons with low-incidence and severe disabilities in school, residential, institutional, and work settings. As a teacher, she developed and implemented systems and plans that supported her middle school students' participation in general education classrooms and in community contexts. Meyer is a long-term collaborator with the University of Oregon's Schools Projects and has participated on design groups for project products. She was an instructor in preservice courses. She also helped design, conduct, transcribe, and analyze interviews with teachers and family members as part of her research projects. Meyer can be reached at Specialized Training Program, 1235 University of Oregon, Eugene, OR 97403-1235; phone: 541-346-2494; fax: 541-346-2471; e-mail: gwenmey@oregon.uoregon.edu.

Ginevra Ralph was an instructor and research assistant in special education and an assistant to the director of Academic Support and Student Services in the College of Education at the University of Oregon. She has collaborated on the University of Oregon's Schools Projects since 1986, working first as a middle school teacher of students with severe disabilities, then as field experiences coordinator, instructor, and grant coordinator for the project's personnel preparation program. She served on state advisory committees in the areas of licensure redesign and innovative professional development efforts and coordinated a professional development grant supporting both general and special educators to increase their abilities to work with a broader range of students. She is currently Director of the American Music Institute, Oregon Festival of American Music. Ralph can be reached at Oregon Festival of American Music, P.O. Box 11254, Eugene, OR 97403-1543; phone: 541-346-6526; gralph@ofam.net.

Nadia Sampson is a research assistant in special education at the University of Oregon. She received her Bachelor of Arts degree in Human Services, and Master's degree in Special Education, and Severely Handicapped Learner Endorsement at the University of Oregon. She spent six years working with survivors of abuse in Oregon, many of whom were people with disabilities. Since 1995, Sampson has been a collaborator on a variety of research projects at the University of Oregon's School Projects. She currently works as the coordinator for the National Institute for Urban School Improvement's resource workgroups and collaborates with other project staff on developing and expanding the institute's Web site resource database on inclusion and urban schooling. Sampson can be reached at Specialized Training Program, 1235 University of Oregon, Eugene, OR 97403-1235; phone: 541-346-2478; fax: 541-346-2471; e-mail: nkatul@oregon.uoregon.edu.

Janet Williams has been teaching for 20 years in general education and special education at the elementary through high school levels. She has held various positions, including special education teacher and consultant, job coordinator and supervisor, elementary teacher for grades K–3, school counselor, mentor, and college instructor. She has worked with students representing a range of diversity in cultural backgrounds, social and economic classes, interests, and abilities, including those students with the most significant disabilities. She currently works for the Basic School Network as an educational consultant/mentor and teaches education courses at D'Youville College in Buffalo, New York. Williams can be reached at 232 Rivermist Drive, Buffalo, NY 14202; phone: 716-854-0591; e-mail: janet@buffnet.net.

If you like this book, you'll LOVE the membership!